ATHEIST TO ENLIGHTENED IN 90 DAYS

Featuring the Equilibrium Diet

Katie Grace Player, Ph.D.

BALBOA.
PRESS
A DIVISION OF HAY HOUSE

Balboa Press books may be ordered through booksellers or by contacting:

Balboa Press
A Division of Hay House
1663 Liberty Drive
Bloomington, IN 47403
www.balboapress.com
1 (877) 407-4847

Print information available on the last page.

ISBN: 978-1-5043-6902-2 (sc)
ISBN: 978-1-5043-6903-9 (hc)
ISBN: 978-1-5043-6901-5 (e)

Library of Congress Control Number: 2016918425

Balboa Press rev. date: 11/15/2016

Contents

Preface

Modern society favors easy and pill-popping fixes; enlightenment and health are neither. This is for the part of you that yearns to *know*, to experience and *not* just believe.

At first, I hesitated to use the word "enlightened" in the title of this book because of the strength, power, and connotations associated with the word enlightenment. Then I remembered a quote by the Buddha: "Achieving enlightenment is easy; it is remaining enlightened that requires work." The former applies to this book while I am still working on the latter—and, as you will see, the title wasn't up to *me*. This story is a bridge—a bridge from one side of your brain to the other—from the left brain to the right brain, from the logical and the rational to the primitive, the intuitive, and the instinctual. This bridge connects science and spirituality; it connects what some call God or Goddess or Creator or Universe with the physical world. It reawakens the instincts and knowledge that ancient people understood and held dear.

For a long time, for years, I was afraid of what people would think of my experience, and I was afraid of what I had discovered—I was afraid of the instincts I had unleashed when I returned to true physical health after a life of disease, weight issues, and the struggle to simply survive. After major dietary changes and the creation of the Equilibrium Diet, I was able to access information I never dreamed possible. And yet once I was able to feel the information—to sense it—I couldn't imagine life without it. It was so simple. I wondered how science had missed it for so long. Humans have instincts just like animals, but somehow, through a combination of poor diet, food additives, environmental toxins, and the era of logic, we have forgotten the basic instincts not just needed to survive but to thrive.

The most common question I am asked after telling my story is, "Why you? Why did an atheist economist get to experience enlightenment?" At first I did not know, but then I realized that I was so left-brained, so analytical, and so in denial regarding spirituality that I would never have believed the experience had it happened to anyone other than me. I also believe I am one of the first of *many*.

This is a full-disclosure book; I have held nothing back. My medical records, blood tests, and pictures of my husband and me that literally track our health are available on my website, www.equilibriumdiet.com. I have included as much evidence as possible in this book and on the website. Where necessary, I have changed the names of some of the people I interacted with to maintain their privacy.

I owe my courage and self-acceptance to brave souls like Wayne Dyer, Caroline Myss, Debbie Ford, and Neale Donald Walsch. Each of these brave, wonderful authors broke through the mold of social stereotypes and acceptable writing experiences. Reading their words helped me feel less alone—less different—and helped me to accept and understand the amazing world I had discovered and what I was here to help others understand. Thank you to each of these Otherselves—I am eternally grateful. As I edited this book, exactly two years after completing the original manuscript, I was once again amazed and awed at how far my family had come, how much transformation had occurred, and the journey we lived during those first few years of health. I am both humbled and honored that for whatever reason, we all chose for me to live this particular vessel and tell this story in this giant game of creation.

The world has not been ready for a diet this powerful until now. I am ready, you are ready—society is ready. Let's experience the amazing creations of which we are truly capable. What I cover in this book is only the tip of the iceberg when it comes to tapping into our human potential. I know that people willing to try the ninety-day detoxification program and adopt the Equilibrium Diet will have experiences far more amazing than those recorded on these pages. Understand this book is not an end-all, be-all; it simply provides a stepping-stone, a foundation or beginning, but it is just that—the beginning.

Introduction

Hello there. You don't think that you know me right now, but you do. I am that ancient part of you that wonders what lies beyond this earthly world. I am the part of you that thinks this world, this life, is all there is. At the same time, I am that part of you that knows there is so much more than just this life—we are all one and the same.

This is the story of an atheist—a pragmatic economist—accidentally becoming enlightened. I never sought enlightenment or believed it to be a possibility; nevertheless, because of the dietary and lifestyle changes I made, enlightenment happened. This is not the story of a near-death experience or physical trauma; it is quite the opposite. Not once but twice I experienced different levels of enlightenment along with daily interactions with the "energy world." Everything in the world and universe is energy, vibrating at different speeds. As humans become healthy, we become sensitive, and what appears to be the physical world gives way to the universe's true energetic nature. Physical boundaries blur, and everything swirls together.

For years I suffered from chronic fatigue, asthma, candida overgrowth, eczema, and an inability to lose weight. After creating the Equilibrium Diet, I overcame every disease I ever had; in addition, my mind and spirit began to balance too. I reawakened the instincts ancient people had, the instincts many primitive tribes and animals still have, and I became a human lie detector. This is quite literally a sixth sense. It is the ability to feel energies outside of our physical bodies—like a storm coming, the toxicity of a plant, or someone's emotions.

I suppose I should start at the beginning. This story begins in July 2010 in Greenville, South Carolina—the middle of the Bible Belt. I had quit my job as an investment-banking analyst to pursue my passion—economics. I was finishing up my PhD in economics at Clemson University. In college, I played volleyball and graduated summa cum laude with majors in economics and finance. My husband, Lance, played baseball in college and was a banker. We were two very ordinary Americans—we had a dog, Theodore, a twenty-two-pound Pomeranian, and we were overweight, tired, and got sick a lot. We ate the standard American diet of wheat, sugar, processed food, and alcohol. Lance's favorite lunch consisted of two Wendy's bacon-cheeseburgers with just ketchup, french fries, and sweet tea. I had his order memorized from countless trips to the drive-through.

But then it all changed. One day in July, Lance, then twenty-five years old, got sick—really sick—and the doctors he saw could not figure out what was wrong with him. That is when I got frustrated. That is when I started asking questions and really *wanting* answers. I discovered we were *both* nutritionally bankrupt, and I started doing my own research and began searching for an equilibrium diet. As an economist, I knew there had to be a way of eating, a way of living, that would provide the body with everything it needed to maintain health. In economic terms, I saw this equilibrium everywhere—I looked at nature and saw plants and animals and even people who never got sick. I knew there had to be a way to replicate this. So I searched, and I found. I never found an equilibrium diet in all of the diets on the market because every diet was flawed in some way. But I had an eye for what worked, and I had the time and patience to test it.

Slowly, gradually, I took the best subsets of many of the better diets on the market and combined them with scientific knowledge of digestion and my instincts—what I will explain later as *vibrational nutrition*—to generate the Equilibrium Diet. After ninety days of internal cleansing and dietary changes, I had my first enlightenment experience—I went from an adamant atheist to a confused spiritualist in an instant; my atheistic reality was shattered, and I was left looking at the pieces. It took months to process and accept that an energetic door had been opened, and my life would be forever changed.

Initially, I did not want to tell anyone about what I had experienced—I was too afraid of what people would say and of what they would think because I knew what I would have thought only months earlier. For years, I lived in a quiet world of isolation, thinking that no one could ever accept my secret and the vibrational world I had discovered. I told myself that I was happy, that I was content. But then I learned there would be no peace for me until I accepted the path the Universe had chosen for me—the path that I had chosen for myself long before I forgot my truth in the physical world of fear, ego, and illusion.

This is the story of relaxing my stubbornness, my rationality, and of giving up the struggle. I finally stopped resisting what I was apparently on earth to do—only then did I calm my inner angst and find peace. In the process, I got out of my own selfish, fearful way and realized that this story wasn't for me—it was for you. It is a blueprint to share with you so that you can discover your own story, your own true self—it is a blueprint to *remembering*. This story is ultimately a challenge. It is a challenge *to* you *from* you to remember who you really are, to *experience* and to *know*. To all people: the religious, the atheist, and the scientist—who are equally faithful to their own set of beliefs—I ask you:

What if you had the chance to prove to yourself—to know—whether or not your current belief system is the truth? Would you embrace that opportunity?

It is bold to suggest a diet can lead you to enlightenment, and yet, that is exactly my proposition—ninety days. Ninety days is all it takes to know. What could you do for ninety days if you knew it meant knowing—if you knew it meant finding your true self? Aren't you worth it? I *know* you are.

* * *

This story unfolds through massive shifts in consciousness. Part 1 begins with the health crisis Lance and I faced and then proceeds to my methodology in creating the Equilibrium Diet. Our health improvements are recorded, including overcoming every health issue either of us ever had: chronic fatigue, candida overgrowth, eczema, prostatitis, asthma, excess weight, and gallbladder disease. I then introduce you to my thought processes and the person I was before our dietary changes and before enlightenment. Then comes the story of the enlightenment experiences and their aftermath, including the realization of my awakened instincts and vibrational nutrition. Part 2 covers the cleansing program and the Equilibrium Diet. Part 2 walks you through everything you need to know to recreate the conditions for this experiment and concludes with a template for you to create your own ninety-day Equilibrium Program. Sometimes I will refer to Source or God or Goddess, as Universe or Divine. This will always be denoted as *Universe* or *Divine*, instead of universe or divine.

I hope you are so provoked, so moved, so angry, or so fearful of what you read on these pages that you decide to discover the edge of your existence—to remember your truth or to prove me wrong; in either case, I dare you to try.

PART I

Atheist to Enlightened in 90 Days

CHAPTER 1

The Health Crisis: Candida Overgrowth

Candida overgrowth consists of an overabundance of *Candida albicans*, opportunistic yeast that colonize the large (and small) intestine when the beneficial flora of the colon are destroyed through antibiotics, an acidifying diet, heavy metal poisoning, environmental toxins, or some combination of these. Foods that acidify the body include refined flours and rice, sugars, preservatives and processed foods, in addition to most meats, eggs, and beans. Candida is the main strand of yeast present in vaginal yeast infections, white-coated tongues, gallbladder problems, and prostatitis, as well as a whole host of other immune problems like chronic fatigue. Until very recently, modern medicine has not recognized or diagnosed candida overgrowth.

* * *

I was a year away from finishing my PhD in economics at Clemson University in South Carolina. At the time, Lance and I were "normal" young Americans; we ate fast food and drank beer with friends and saw medical doctors when we were sick. We thought it was normal to take an antibiotic two or three times a year for sinus infections and to pop Tylenol when we had headaches or body aches. As former college athletes, we were accustomed to taking hydrocodone for severe pain, Lamisil for athlete's foot, and antihistamines for seasonal allergies. In college, we both had strict schedules and little free time, so when we graduated and found ourselves tired and sleepy, we attributed it to being out of "college athlete shape" and getting older. We thought that grinding through life and responsibilities loaded up on caffeine and sugar was how life was managed. When we had time off or took vacation, we slept a lot—we were generally exhausted.

In early July, Lance came home early on a Friday from work. Within moments, he confessed that he didn't feel well. Lance said he had severe stabbing pain below his ribcage in his right abdomen. I was familiar with appendicitis and knew that in some cases people could have referred pain, so I immediately thought Lance's appendix might be causing the pain. Lance could not take a deep breath the pain was so severe, and he agreed to let me drive him to a late-hours doctors' clinic. We arrived at the clinic several minutes later, and the doctor poked and prodded and ran a urine analysis.

The doctor looked to be a first-year resident or younger. She said Lance's appendix was fine but that he had kidney stones. The doctor said it wasn't uncommon and that Lance's pain ran all the way up his ureter; therefore, his pain must be caused by kidney stones. She referred him to a urologist and sent us away with painkillers and antinausea pills. Lance had already been seeing a urologist for prostatitis for years. I was not thrilled about going back to his urologist, because at our last meeting, she quite literally laughed in my face when I asked if Lance's prostatitis could be due to a male yeast infection. I told her that his symptoms seemed to be cyclical and coincided with when I had yeast infections. His symptoms got worse at night—which is also typical of yeast infections, and yeast is highly contagious. The doctor was not concerned; she just said no, that men didn't get yeast infections. And I didn't ask her any more questions during the visit.

Within days we were at Lance's urologist's office and getting nowhere fast. The urologist ruled out kidney stones with a CT scan, and for the next two weeks, Lance was bounced around from specialist to specialist, given more and more drugs, and getting progressively worse—no doctor could identify what was wrong. Finally, he was given a diagnosis of Crohn's disease and sent home with a pamphlet labeled "Living with Crohn's." Crohn's disease is considered a rare chronic inflammatory illness characterized by inflamed intestines, stomach pain, weight loss, diarrhea, and sometimes fatigue.

Lance lost fifteen pounds in those initial weeks because he was so nauseous that he barely ate. Prior to this episode, I thought Lance was in pretty good shape. We both enjoyed fast food every week or so, but in general, I *thought* we ate well—after all, I cooked the majority of our dinners. Lance did not exercise regularly anymore, and he had a few pounds to lose, but he really didn't have fifteen pounds to lose.

After Lance's second weekend of not getting off the couch, and me becoming increasingly frustrated with the medical community's lack of urgency, I thought, *Enough is enough. I'm a problem-solver—I'll figure it out.* That's when I started asking questions and really *wanting* answers. I began compiling what I knew at very fundamental levels, and I started researching nutrition. I used the following questions and facts to stimulate my research.

1. Why is a formerly healthy twenty-five-year-old athletic male having such health problems?
2. I know Lance currently has prostatitis. The prostate and the appendix are both very low blood-flow areas.
3. Blood is what nourishes our body and our cells; our blood is what feeds everything in us.
4. Lance's blood must not be nutritious enough to feed and cleanse the low blood-flow areas. For whatever reason, by the time his blood arrives, it is not potent enough to do its job.

I deduced that nutrition had to play a part. The first thing I thought about were parasites—parasites make it tough for blood to do its job, because they consume the body's resources. I started researching parasites and parasitic infections. I found a possible cause: sushi. Lance loved sushi and sometimes ate it twice a day. Liver flukes are parasites that can be found in raw seafood and can cause a host of bodily problems. In the middle of researching parasites, I discovered that heavy metal poisoning can be another precursor to disease in people who consume large amounts of fish. I had two topics to research further: anti-parasite programs and heavy metal removal, which is usually referred to as chelation.

I read about parasites and anti-parasite programs and learned that modern medicine had virtually nothing to offer in terms of effective parasite treatment. This was confirmed by a colleague of Lance's who had battled parasites from raw oysters years earlier. Lance's colleague ended up healing himself with herbs when the medical doctors told him there was nothing they could do for his parasites and bloody stool. He let us borrow his book, *Nutritional Healing from A–Z,* by Phyllis A. Balch, CNC. He had highlighted all of the herbs and supplements used to treat parasites.

Lance and I began reading through the enormous book, and then I went to a place I had never been before—Garner's, the local herb store. I bought two herbal parasite cleanses, one for Lance and one for myself. I didn't like sushi, but I figured that I had better take one too—in case the critters were contagious. The day Lance went to see a general surgeon, he began taking anti-parasite herbs. Both of us eliminated processed food and sugar from our diet, because I read that anything that was quickly converted to glucose fed parasites—I thought that seemed logical.

Lance had scheduled himself an appointment with a general surgeon; he wanted to talk to a generalist instead of more specialists. Lance's appointment with the general surgeon was the most productive appointment he'd had with a doctor in weeks. The surgeon identified the pain as Lance's gallbladder and wanted to run tests to be 100 percent sure the gallbladder was the problem before removing it. The surgeon scheduled Lance for a tentative gallbladder surgery date in mid-September. Before the surgery, Lance was scheduled for a hepatobiliary scan (HIDA scan) to test the gallbladder's functionality, a colonoscopy, and an endoscopy. The latter two procedures were to narrow out Crohn's disease. I would later learn that holistic doctors and natural healers would usually target candida overgrowth as the main imbalance leading to Crohn's disease.

The tests were scheduled, but after one day on the anti-parasite herbs, Lance felt good enough to get off the couch and start moving around. After three days of taking the herbs, Lance was almost 100 percent better—with the exception of not wanting to eat much—and he returned to work. The only tests he ended up having were an ultrasound, which came up negative for any gallstones, and the HIDA scan. In a HIDA scan, the patient is injected with a radioactive tracer that is monitored after the liver removes the tracer from the blood and is encouraged to "dump" it into the bile and small intestine when injected with copious amounts of fat. The large amounts of fat ensure the gallbladder will at least try to eject bile. A gamma wave camera tracks the radiation throughout the process. The HIDA scan showed that Lance's gallbladder was functioning at about 70 percent. We were told the medical standard for gallbladder removal required a functionality at or below 30 percent—unless, of course, the patient is in pain and wants the gallbladder removed.

Never was there any discussion with the doctor about the problems people face when the gallbladder is removed and they are left to digest foods without a gallbladder. None of the doctors or nurses ever mentioned the fact that the gallbladder stores bile, and bile is needed to digest fats. The medical practitioners never talked about how people without gallbladders will never be able to eat like they did before surgery since the liver is then forced to produce bile on command. (The liver cannot produce bile on command, other than a very small amount that could potentially be stored in the bile duct between the liver and duodenum. This is why when a person without a gallbladder eats a fatty meal, he has to run to the bathroom. The fat in the meal cannot be digested and is treated as toxic material by the body. The body wants to get it out as quickly as possible.) Fat-soluble vitamins cannot be absorbed without bile in the cases of animal fat, olive oil, and coconut oil. Vitamins A, D, and E are necessary for so many bodily functions and reproduction. Weston A. Price, DDS, documented studies and pictures of animals born when the mother was fed a diet low in vitamin A or E, and each case resulted in excessive birth defects and usually stillbirths[1].

But at that time, the tests and doctors and potential surgeries seemed perfectly normal to Lance and me. Looking back, I shake my head about willingly ingesting radioactive particles and then sitting under more radiation for ninety minutes while a camera tracks the radiation moving through your system. But this was the model Lance and I grew up with—we did not know any other way; we had no knowledge of alternative models for comparison. We had constrained ourselves with the norms of our family, our history, and our society—to our own detriment.

After beginning the anti-parasite herbs, we started to eat healthier, took a lot of raw garlic, and I kept reading. I discovered that my rational instinct about our blood not being nutritious enough was dead on. I discovered that not only Lance but both of us had all of the symptoms of full-fledged candida overgrowth, a condition recognized by the medical community only for patients with severe autoimmune disorders. I learned that my need to sleep twelve hours a night and take a two-hour nap during the day was *not* normal. I never felt rested or refreshed from sleep. I learned that candida overgrowth can cause the imbalance behind medical diagnoses like chronic fatigue, prostatitis, Crohn's disease, gallbladder problems, and a host of other illnesses. With few formal candida tests and the medical community's general dismissal of the imbalance, I knew we would be on our own.

I began by having Lance and myself list all of our symptoms and health issues. Lance listed acute symptoms of weight loss, sick after eating, no appetite, nausea, back pain, and sharp abdomen pain and then the additional chronic symptoms.

Lance's Chronic Symptoms

Prostatitis	Athlete's foot	Seasonal allergies
Fatigue	Neck/shoulder muscle pain	Itchy genital area
Tired after meals	Sinus problems	Stringy saliva—in water glass

As an infant, Lance had constant ear infections starting at six weeks of age. He took antibiotics on and off and had tubes in his ears on many occasions; he was allergic to casein, the protein that constitutes 80 percent of the protein in dairy products. Lance struggled with ear infections his entire life due to his dairy intolerance. He was also on an antibiotic at least twice a year for sinus infections.

Lance had been struggling with prostatitis for five years. He had been on high-powered antibiotics for close to six months in college for it, and his most recent medication was Toviaz, a bladder medication aimed at shrinking the size of his bladder to give his enlarged and painful prostate "more room." The doctor thought this powerful drug would alleviate the problems Lance had with his prostate. During the entire five-year period, the doctors never mentioned the possible side effects of any of the drugs, nor the possibility of a change in diet. Instead, Lance's prostate was inflamed and enlarged, and the medical solution was to try to shrink his bladder instead of finding out what was *causing* the inflammation and enlargement of the prostate. The equivalent of this thinking would be to take your leaking boat, with a huge gaping hole in the floor to a boat repair shop, and instead of fixing the hole and solidifying the structure, the repairman simply throws out all of your life jackets and furniture in the boat to make room for more water. Sure, it might actually work for a while, maybe it buys you some time and space—but you are still sinking.

After reviewing my own symptom list and realizing that I'd had chronic fatigue for over two years, I was faced with the realization that I was unhealthy too—I listed the following symptoms:

Constant headache	Tinnitus (ringing in the ears)	Tired after meals
Non-refreshing sleep	Brain fog	Scratchy throat
Skin lesions	Itchy genital area	Migraines
Sinus congestion	Chest congestion	Seasonal allergies
Fatigue (11+ hours of sleep)	Sharp, fleeting chest pains	Dull skull pain
Tight neck/ shoulder muscles	Swollen, painful lymph nodes	Decreased peripheral vision

Additionally, I had tingling on the side of my left eye down to my left lower lip along the jaw muscle, my breasts ached near the lymph nodes, the bottoms of my feet itched like crazy but nothing seemed to be on them, and I had a basal body temperature of 96.0 degrees (indicative of hypothyroidism). I also had stringy saliva when I spit into a glass of water (an easy candida test). And most of my symptoms seemed to get worse with sugar consumption.

As a toddler, I was hospitalized for asthma attacks, and I continued to keep two inhalers around for wheezing problems and to prevent sinus infections from entering my lungs. As far back as I can remember, I took at least two rounds of antibiotics per year for a sinus infection or strep throat. In high school and college, I had horrible, itchy contact dermatitis and eczema. The dermatologist prescribed me a high-power steroid cream (Ultravate), which I used regularly. I found out after years of using it that it was also a skin thinner and was known to cause cancer in rats. The dermatologist had me using it on my eyelids when my eczema flared.

Reviewing our symptoms list was a wake-up call for both of us. We were both in pretty rough shape. We realized something had to change for our health to improve, but we didn't really know what yet. I kept digging. I went on a research rampage and for weeks worked almost around the clock to study nutrition, candida, and diets. I discovered juice fasting (no solid foods, only juice), which made sense to me because when animals are sick—they fast. Digestion is the largest energetic expense in the body—it consumes 80 percent of our energy. There are times when we need to free up that energy to do other things like clean, repair, and rebuild. Lance and I decided to do a juice fast to reduce the digestive burden on our bodies and to give our livers some time to "repair" in needed areas. We didn't know how it would go or what to expect, but we did it anyway. Unbeknownst to us at the time, the juice fast would provide the drastic break from the standard American diet that we would need to sustain a new healthy lifestyle indefinitely.

* * *

I did an eleven-day juice fast, and Lance did a three-day fast. We did not consume any solid food during the fast—we only drank raw vegetable and fruit juices and vegetable broths. We had never felt better, and it was a life-changing experience because we realized how good life can actually feel. Surprisingly, I lost one pound in eleven days of fasting, but I lost two clothing sizes. I dropped to a size 4 from a size 8—over the next month of eating well, I dropped to a size 2! Lance dropped to a size 32 from a size 36 and lost five more pounds during the first six months of our dietary changes.

How is it possible to lose so little weight but drop so many inches? Have you ever seen someone who just looks puffy or bloated—like the texture of a mushroom? That's how I looked before the fast. Then I lost all of the junk my body was holding onto because it hadn't had time to clean and deal with all of the new bad stuff I was constantly consuming. The data collector that I am, I had blood tests done before and after the juice fast for comparison, and I continued to monitor my blood over the next several years. (See www.equilibriumdiet.com for copies of my blood work and medical records.)

The first twenty-four hours of the fast were the most difficult. During this period, the liver doesn't yet realize that it doesn't have to get ready to digest more food. Once the liver realizes it can actually go to work on old projects and repairs, it starts cleaning, and you are no longer concerned with food and eating. I was the hungriest during those first twenty-four hours; it wasn't terrible—I just wanted to eat at my normal times for breakfast, lunch, and dinner. I kept my mind busy and off of food; this was important because I did not want to be dwelling on things I could not have. The last nine days were much easier, with the exception of a few rough hours when some heavy detoxification occurred—fasting books warn that during a fast you will relive every illness you have ever had. This releasing of past trauma typically occurs in a matter of minutes or hours. I relived the flu virus for several hours and an old high school basketball knee injury. But, in general, I had more energy than I normally did, my sinuses were clearer, my thoughts were clearer, and I slept much more soundly.

After the juice fast, we completely cut out all processed food, preservatives, refined flour, and sugar and began to explore the anti-candida diet. The diet recommends consuming high amounts of proteins and low amounts of carbohydrates. Sugar of all kinds is eliminated. All fruits are to be avoided with the exception of Granny Smith apples because of the sugar content. Even sugar in spaghetti sauce was eliminated. It was a major lifestyle change and paid off immediately.

The initial two weeks without any sugar or processed food were hard because of the cravings. All of the bad stuff dying in my body was screaming out to be fed, telling me to eat processed pizza and cake and candy and soda. But once it was dead and gone, the thought of sugar was repulsing. This was much easier for me than for Lance because most of my "critters" had died in the long juice fast. It really takes about thirty to forty days without sugar and processed food to starve off the majority of parasites, yeasts, and viruses. After the eleven-day fast, I had sugar cravings for about two weeks—Lance had them for a month after his three-day fast. Lance and I never followed the anti-candida diet strictly, because even at first glance and without much nutritional knowledge, the diet seemed flawed to me. There were several major problems with the diet:

1. It was very similar to the Atkins diet and Paleo diet in that it recommended eating large amounts of protein. Even given my limited knowledge at the time, I knew the body couldn't handle high levels of protein for extended periods of time. Because of this, the anti-candida diet was not an equilibrium diet; that is, it could not be healthily sustained for a lifetime. (Eventually I learned that high levels of protein cause stress on the body, particularly the liver and kidneys.)
2. The anti-candida diet eliminated almost all fruits. I found fruits to be an essential part of a nutritious diet, particularly in the summertime, so I didn't see cutting out fruits on a long-term basis. It was not an equilibrium.
3. The anti-candida diet did not provide a self-sustaining amount of nutrients to the body; neither did the Atkins diet.

* * *

On a trip to Charleston that September, we met with a friend, Steve, for dinner. Steve is an Italian American whose grandmother immigrated to New York City from Italy. Lance had not had any pain or gallbladder problems since beginning the anti-parasite herbs almost a month earlier, but his past gallbladder problems somehow came up in conversation. Steve told us the remedy that his Italian grandmother had recommended to him when the doctors suggested Steve have his gallbladder removed.

He said, "In Italy and later in New York, my grandmother would drink olive oil mixed with lemon juice right before going to bed at night and again first thing in the morning. It's called a gallbladder flush or a liver flush, and it keeps stones from forming in the gallbladder. I did it twenty years ago—and I still do it if I ever have gallbladder pain—and I never had my gallbladder removed because it worked so well. My grandmother recommended it for everything—nausea, allergies, chronic illness; she would tell you to go drink some olive oil and lemon juice."

Lance and I both found the idea interesting, but we weren't sure how to implement it yet, so we just let it marinate in our heads. Then about a week later, our realtor loaned us a book called *The Amazing Liver and Gallbladder Flush,* by Andres Moritz. I had told him of our dietary changes, and he recommended I read it. The book laid out the how-to's of performing a liver flush. After the juice fast, Lance and I figured, "We have nothing to lose but a cup of olive oil and grapefruit juice, and some time—why not try it?" Moritz's recipe was slightly different from the Italian grandmother's recipe, but people seemed to see great results from it.

So we tried it. Actually, that first time, the liver flush absolutely dominated both of us. We woke up at 3:00 a.m. after drinking the olive oil and grapefruit juice mixture to nausea so extreme we both lay on the cool bathroom tile and just moaned for hours. In those moments, we thought it was the worst thing either of us had ever done in our lives.

The next morning, we expelled over two thousand liver stones plus even more cholesterol crystals between the two of us—oh yes, we counted! We learned that the nausea occurs when the liver dumps so many stones that the stones get backed up into the stomach instead of trickling easily into the small intestine. But after defecating the stones, we felt amazing for weeks. Our bodies were much more flexible, we had more energy, and we could see more clearly. It was well worth the investment of those two hours of nausea in the wee morning hours. Over the next year, we did six more liver flushes; fortunately, we never experienced nausea during any of those subsequent flushes, and we expelled several thousand more stones.

The Purge

About thirty days into our dietary changes, it was time to purge. I had to throw away all of the foods we would no longer eat. I had a huge pantry full of everything from breakfast cereals to canned soups and vegetables and sauces and cookies. When I looked at the ingredient lists, they were filled with high fructose corn syrup, sugar, yellow 5, monosodium glutamate, and other additives of which I had never heard nor could pronounce.

Some of the food I gave away. That made it easier. But I tossed out a lot. This was part of the emotional cleanse too. I had to let go of my old eating patterns and thought patterns. I had to really rip up and destroy the old habits to make way for the new, clean, nourishing thoughts and foods. It was a purge that had to be completed to truly move forward. The old eating patterns had not paid off, and it was time to let them go. I had made the decision that I was worth the investment of high-quality, nutrient-dense food—even if that meant letting go of the past—even if it meant realigning my budget.

* * *

I continued to search for a sustainable, lifelong way of eating that minimized stress on the body. I looked at the world around me, and I saw healthy equilibriums in nature: plants, animals, even humans living disease-free lives. If this equilibrium level of health existed in nature, it must exist for me—for everyone. How do we create that? I *knew* a vibrant equilibrium had to exist.

CHAPTER 2

Discovering the Equilibrium Diet

Knowing something exists and finding it are two different things. I knew an equilibrium state of health was theoretically possible. I needed to go about identifying it and recreating it. I began the search, looking at various diets. We tried several diets for a while. Raw, vegan, macrobiotic, anti-candida, Paleo, and the Pro-Vita—each had its strengths but also its weaknesses. No diet proved to be an equilibrium. Every existing diet was too prescriptive, too limited, and too costly to the body and the liver to yield a lifetime of vibrant health.

There was so much information available on diet and nutrition, but most of it was contradictory. Many diets focused on minimizing fat intake, but fat-soluble vitamins are needed for many things, including the reproductive and immune systems. I quickly recognized the contradictions, and I knew I needed to develop a method for sifting through the massive amounts of information. At the outset, I approached getting healthy like any other economic problem. I told myself, "I don't care what people say even if they are specialists or so-called nutritional experts—I care what healthy people *do*. I need to see the data; I need to identify very healthy people." I knew that I could then work backwards and figure out what created extremely healthy people.

All of my research focused on three questions:

1) What is equilibrium health?
2) Who are the healthiest people in the world?
3) How do the healthiest people live and eat?

When I first began searching for an equilibrium way of eating, my thought process was governed by economic reasoning, statistics, and my basic understanding of how digestion and the body worked. I knew that to identify an equilibrium lifestyle, I would first have to identify *health*. I further focused my research on several sub-questions:

1. How did our ancient ancestors eat?
2. Is there anything we know scientifically that aids or hinders digestion?
3. As a mini-economy, what are the costs and benefits the body faces in digestion?

What is equilibrium health?

Health is vibrant—health is energy—health gleams. All of these are difficult parameters to find and measure. So I defined health as the lack of disease and the lack of imbalance. This is not easily found in America. This means no allergies, no fatigue, no depression, no headaches, no heartburn, no PMS, the absence of all OTC and pharmaceutical medications, no heart/liver/lung/gallbladder/prostate/uterus problems. I could not think of a single person I knew personally who fit this description of health. I needed to look beyond the people I knew and interacted with on a daily basis.

Who are the healthiest people in the world?

The next step was identifying healthy groups of people. Seventh Day Adventists, the Japanese, and rural Sicilians are population segments known to have statistically better health outcomes than average Americans. However, I found that the most robust health was in Buddhist monks and primitive tribes still untouched by modern society. I came to this conclusion after seeing many pictures of Buddhist monks and primitive tribesmen who were over ninety years old with gleaming faces and virtually no wrinkles. I recognized that primitive tribes are the closest living example of how our ancient ancestors would have eaten. Neither the monks nor the tribesmen had been adulterated by white flour, processed food, or sugar.

I asked myself, "What do these people do differently? What and how do they eat?"

The important aspects of the Buddhist and primitive diet seemed to be summarized by the following concepts.

1. The complete absence of processed food and sugar in both groups.
2. Both groups eat their largest meal for breakfast.
3. Buddhist monks are typically vegetarians; primitive tribes are *rarely* vegetarian.

Primitive peoples go through extensive souring or fermenting processes before eating grains and legumes. Buddhist monks do not eat anything for dinner and usually do not eat past the noon meal. I combined this information with my experiential findings that Lance seemed to have gallbladder attacks at night after eating protein-heavy meals. Lance did not have gallbladder attacks when he ate meats and proteins in the morning, even eggs and nuts, which are known for triggering gallbladder attacks.

My suspicion regarding the importance of the timing of when we eat certain foods was confirmed when I learned about the pH cycle of the body in *The Pro-Vita Diet* by Jack Tipps, ND. The body needs to be in an acidic state to properly digest proteins; this occurs naturally before 2:00 p.m. The body is most acidic between 6:00 a.m. and 7:30 a.m. Proteins take four to eight hours to digest, with plant sources being the easiest and fastest to digest and red meat and pork the longest and most difficult.

Avoiding proteins after 2:00 p.m. allows the liver to spend time cleaning and repairing while we sleep instead of spending energy on digestion. I found that this resonated with me intuitively, so we adopted it. We began eating our largest meal, dense in proteins, for breakfast and avoiding protein after 2:00 p.m. We discovered that when we ate four to five different sources of protein at both breakfast and lunch that by dinner time we were still so full we could barely eat a piece of fruit. We were never hungry, except before breakfast. Our blood sugar had completely stabilized along with our moods. My lifelong symptoms of hypoglycemia disappeared virtually overnight.

Next, I read about the healing wonders of raw and living foods. Raw fruits and vegetables are in their most natural state, so it made sense that primitive tribes and our ancestors may have simply plucked fruits and vegetables and consumed them raw. During the first several months of our dietary changes, I ate most of my fruits and vegetables raw. The raw foods did an excellent job of cleaning and purging the body. (Raw foods provide fiber and roughage, which bind to toxic material.) At first, I thought that the raw foods diet was the answer—I was wrong. After several months of eating mostly raw vegetables,

I began noticing large amounts of undigested food in my stool. I found myself craving cooked foods. It seemed I wasn't getting many nutrients from the raw foods I was eating. My body had ended its cleansing cycle and was ready to build.

I started listening to my body and began eating cooked vegetables. I felt immediately better. I had broken away from the path of all standard diets and nutritional advice. This was the beginning of what I refer to as *vibrational nutrition.* I realized that the standard approaches to nutrition were too constrained to yield optimum health and that humans, like the planet, cycle with the seasons. I began to track my body's cycles, urges, and nutritional demands. The urge to cleanse with raw foods would always be followed by the urge to build with mineral-rich foods like red meat, lobster, crab, and greens. Not surprisingly, I found that the more I ate according to my instincts, the more my instincts aligned with seasonal changes. In some seasons, we need to be warmed and strengthened, whereas in others we need to be cooled and cleaned. We cannot be truly healthy by endlessly repeating the same cycle.

* * *

The Economics of Digestion

Fact: The biggest cost to the human body is digestion; the human body spends approximately 80 percent of its energy on digestive processes. Over the past 150 years, Western society has driven itself into nutritional bankruptcy.

After studying various diets and the science of digestion, I connected everything with my understanding of economics. After all, pristine health is simply the output of a well-organized digestive strategy, one where the food consumed yields high returns on the digestive cost needed to undertake each meal. The human body is like any other ecosystem or business or economy. It's comprised of millions of individual agents trying to do the best they can for themselves with some limited number of resources. If the body or the business crashes, it is for two reasons: it has not adapted to change, and it has inferior inputs and processes—the two reasons are usually intertwined. Most people in the Western world today are in a state of what I call nutritional bankruptcy—the quality of the food they consume is so low, and their digestive processes are so weak from years of nutrients being stripped away, that they have no nutritional reserves left to use when it comes time to digest a meal or fight off an illness.

They are beyond empty and therefore lack the energy and nutrients needed to keep the body clean. Thus, toxins accumulate to eat the waste the body has not dealt with, and disease sets in. Nutritional bankruptcy occurs when the costs of digestion have exceeded the nutrients derived from meals for an extended period of time. The Equilibrium Diet purges the systems of the body, improves the body's processes, and provides high-quality nutrients (inputs) so nutritional bankruptcy is eliminated.

When you improve the input qualities and processes, you get a more efficient business—you get a more efficient body—you get "more bang for your buck"—and you get *healthy*. Digestion is what economists and businesses call a "fixed cost"; no matter what type of food you eat, you pay the same price in digestive juices, enzymes, and cellular energy. This is slightly oversimplified because the fixed cost could be approximated with the cost of digesting fruit, whereas the digestive cost increases with more complex structures like fats and proteins. Regardless, there is a fixed cost of all digestion that represents the minerals and amino acids needed to properly break down foods. To receive a positive return on the body's investment in digestive processes, you *must* consume foods that contain at least as many nutrients as it costs the body to digest the food.

If you eat foods with lower nutritional value than the cost of digestion, the body pulls from its current reserves in your bones, your tendons, and your organs. This is a stopgap process and cannot go on for long periods of time; the cost will *always* be paid—there is no free lunch. This is why sugar, refined flour, white rice, and processed foods are detrimental to the body; none of these foods provide enough nutrients to cover the digestive cost of eating them. When the benefits do not exceed the costs for an extended period of time, we end up *nutritionally bankrupt*. Thankfully, just like our wallets, once we begin to work with the body to improve its inputs and processes by eating nutrient-dense foods, the body begins to return to its natural state: vitality—physical, mental, and *spiritual* vitality. We can think of the Equilibrium Diet as a protocol for restoring, improving, and sorting through our nutritional asset base—a nutritional bankruptcy court, so to speak.

* * *

The Diet

The Equilibrium Diet propelled me out of nutritional bankruptcy and unlocked my instincts, one of which is *vibrational nutrition*—the ability to sense which foods are good for us and bad for us. The diet focuses on utilizing the body's natural cycles to minimize the stress the liver and other organs face. We get healthier just by switching *when* we eat traditional breakfast foods and dinner foods. We do this by avoiding proteins after 2:00 p.m., which aligns protein digestion with the body's acidic pH cycle and sugar/carb digestion with the alkaline portion of the cycle. When the liver is not preoccupied with digestion, it can "go clean"—neutralizing toxins and repairing needed tissues.

Raw foods take a great deal of digestive work *if* you have enough stomach acid and enzymes to digest raw foods *at all*—historically, our ancestors ate vegetables cooked. This means that for most people, almost all vegetables should be cooked to reduce the digestive burden. Essentially, cooking foods reduces the cost to the body of digestion. Raw plant-based diets overlook that the human body must be able to break down the plant to use it. Alfalfa is one of the most nutritious foods on the planet, but humans do not have the digestive rigor to get anything out of it. It takes cows with four stomachs to break alfalfa into usable components. It is true that cooking vegetables compromises some of the vitamin and mineral levels; however, for the vast majority of people, the return on digestive investment for cooked vegetables exceeds that of raw vegetables. This is because humans get very little nutritional value from raw vegetables—we lack the digestive robustness to break down cellulose (the tough fibrous cell walls of plants).

The final component of the Equilibrium Diet was my search for the most mineral-rich foods on the planet—foods that could build up a nutritionally bankrupt body. I needed foods that were not only dense in nutrients but easy for the body to digest as well. I let my own instincts and cravings guide me to *vibrationally* test foods, and the Universe eventually led me to supporting research. I determined that the four best foods for most people to eat are: organ meats, *unpasteurized* dairy, anything from the sea, and fresh raw vegetable juices. These foods yield the highest return on investment given the body's cost to digest them. They provide the biggest nutritional bang for our digestive buck. Each food is relatively easy to digest, particularly compared to its substitutes: muscle meats, pasteurized dairy, animal proteins, and vegetables, respectively.

Each super-food provides vast stores of easily absorbable vitamins and minerals. With each food, the digestive work is minimized or done for you—this implies a low digestive cost packed with high nutrient density. (Please note that many people will not be able to properly digest the casein protein in cows' milk even when unpasteurized. These individuals should rely on raw milks from goats or sheep to minimize the intolerance and reduce inflammation.)

These are the four major food groups that help strengthen and build the body. Without these foods, vitality and a return to health cannot occur. You can cleanse and remove current toxins, and you will feel better, but most people will never be able to rebuild the body's lost stores of nutrients on a solely plant-based or raw diet. This is because the digestive return on plant proteins and nutrients is greatly below the return on organ meats, raw dairy, and seafood. These three foods are the most nutrient dense *and* easily absorbable foods on the planet. Weston A. Price, DDS, studied primitive people and diets and came to the same conclusion: the healthiest people in the world eat an abundance of at least two of the three categories. I have added raw vegetable juices to the list because they are packed with vitamins and minerals and are not very filling. So if someone is looking to build her reserves, she can eat a full meal in addition to drinking a raw juice, which supplies scores of nutrients. Furthermore, raw juices augment our mineral stores, which can be low due to the depleted soil in which modern foods grow.

The Equilibrium Diet is the most nourishing and least stressful way of eating currently available—it is the most efficient way of eating, because it takes into account the digestive cost of eating food. The top priority in this lifestyle is *listening* to *your* body. It will take at least ninety days of detox to relearn how to listen to your body and rediscover your instincts. Because most of us are so far removed from our instincts, the guidelines of the Equilibrium Diet provide a roadmap to rediscovery. Once you climb out of nutritional bankruptcy, once you can listen to yourself, you won't need me or *any* diet ever again.

CHAPTER 3

Radical Changes

Our path toward alternative healing began the day I walked into Garner's and purchased anti-parasite herbs. We continued to shift toward more natural solutions with each step: taking the herbs, fasting, dietary changes, the liver flush, the elimination of all over-the-counter and pharmaceutical drugs. We told three different medical doctors that we had all of the symptoms of candida overgrowth. Each doctor said it wasn't possible, that we didn't have AIDS, so we couldn't have candida. The doctors never explained why we couldn't have candida overgrowth or parasites, even when we asked directly. They just stated, "It's not the case."

When pressed, they said, "Just trust me."

Our health had reached the point where we didn't have the luxury of trust anymore. I asked the doctors about the herbal remedies for candida that I had read about. The medical doctors told us none of it would work and that there'd been no proven research to support herbal remedies and alternative medicine. After three weeks, fifteen pounds, six doctors, and a medical solution of gallbladder removal, I didn't trust anyone but myself. Our journey to alternative medicine had begun, but we had a long road ahead of us. The world of natural medicine is ancient, vast, and overwhelming for the logical mind. In the early days, really the first one to two years, of our road to recovery, we were absolute amateurs in the holistic world.

I was still thinking in an analytical, left-brained, symptom-treating manner, but we had entered the world of energy without realizing it. This caused growing pains for Lance and me. I was trying to operate on the body with herbs like a medical doctor would do with pharmaceutical drugs. I was still focusing on symptom alleviation instead of consciously treating the whole person. Taking herbs to relieve symptoms can and does "force" results—but it isn't permanent. Suffering is minimized when the actual level of the *problem* is addressed instead of just the *symptom*.

I had been ignoring my own body and its voice. I was listening to other people's advice instead of my highest guide—myself. I was a squirrel who didn't know what acorns looked like and gathered everything in case it was, in fact, an acorn. This was horrible in terms of diagnostic precision but wonderful long-term because I accumulated vast amounts of holistic knowledge in a very short amount of time. Because of my inexperience, we bought and took a lot more herbs and remedies than we needed. Inefficiency was the buzzword of our steep learning curve. I was bouncing around from website to website and herbal list to list in an attempt to patch us back together.

I was so new to this herbal model that I didn't know anyone else who used herbs. I didn't even know that natural doctors or homeopaths existed. Once I discovered such alternative healers existed, it was another struggle and search to actually find practitioners in my area. I didn't speak their language yet, so it was tough to find them online. Furthermore, I didn't know what skills I was looking for in a natural doctor because of my limited holistic knowledge and vocabulary. I spent much of those first few months doing my own research, floundering, and making my own small discoveries. In the countless hours of research I did, it is quite amazing that I did not find something earlier that would have led me to a local natural doctor. It was as if the Universe blocked all of that information from me; for some reason, I needed to discover the road to health on my own.

Eventually, I went to a local homeopath two times in that first year when several new friends recommended her. The doctor actually practices "integrated medicine," and I learned that, legally, homeopaths are not allowed in South Carolina, so they end up listed as "integrated doctors" or "chiropractors." This may have been what was driving much of my confusion in terms of searching for herbal and homeopathic practitioners; I was searching for the wrong "person" in South Carolina. This particular integrated doctor introduced me to some of the top naturopath remedy brands like Systemic Formulas, Nutri-West, and SafeCareRX, which would prove to be instrumental in overcoming candida overgrowth. I was not a "good" patient for her because of my own impatience and desire to learn. She wanted me to only use the herbal remedies she was prescribing—understandably. But I was trying to fly instead of learning to crawl first. I was experimenting with different remedies, making it difficult for the holistic doctor to track my progress. I suppose the Universe intervened again; this was a road I needed to travel alone for a while. I could sense the holistic doctor was beginning to get more than a little frustrated with me, so I stopped going after my second visit.

My husband and I struggled and learned and struggled and learned, but we were still operating entirely in our linear left brains. The left brain cannot handle the massive amounts of information needed to make a holistic decision. To efficiently use holistic medicine, the right brain and its power must be embraced and harnessed—every person, every situation, every imbalance is unique. When appropriately implemented, natural medicine does not record a list of symptoms and then prescribe one end-all, be-all drug or herb like most modern medical doctors do. This is the orderly, linear, left-brain approach—noting symptoms, making a probabilistic assumption about the "illness," and then prescribing the drug. True holistic medicine means "wholeness" and nudges the body, mind, and spirit back into balance. Natural medicine focuses on the cause of the imbalance and mending the cause instead of masking a symptom. The cause of imbalance can be a myriad of factors: family relationships, emotions, thought patterns, stress, trauma, environmental toxins, and diet, among others. Rarely will a holistic remedy be identical for two individuals, even if they display similar symptoms.

* * *

After three months of eliminating all sugar and processed foods and avoiding meats after 2:00 p.m., Lance and I felt like completely different people. We both felt great overall and were basking in our improved health, energy levels, and quality of sleep. I was working on my dissertation twelve to fourteen hours a day with no physical or mental strain. The sugar cravings had been gone for months, and all of the goodies around Thanksgiving were downright off-putting. Now that the sugar and processed foods were out of our systems, we had absolutely no desire for even a small bite of a sugary treat. I did notice that when I finally tried one bite of a cookie, the level of sweetness was overwhelming; it was like eating straight sugar, and I did not make that mistake again.

In December, I discovered a Bikram yoga class. Bikram yoga, often referred to as "hot yoga," is a series of yoga postures completed in a room with a temperature of 90–105 degrees. I fell in love with the class because it was relaxing and a great workout. I sweated more in that class than I did in twice-a-day college volleyball practices. During the yoga classes, I started feeling sensations I had never felt before. The only experience it was even remotely close to was dizziness—like that tingling you get in your head, but this was "dizziness" in body parts other than my head. It would get very intense and felt like it was radiating all around me. It was a little like the feeling of a body part waking up from "being asleep" when the circulation is cut off. This was a much milder version and had a consistency to it, almost a hum, and it felt like it was outside of my body instead of inside it. The first few times I felt the energy vibrations, I did not know what was happening. I would try to go to a resting pose until it subsided, but sometimes it wouldn't subside for hours after class. I tried to hydrate and take in lots of extra electrolytes thinking that maybe the sensations were due to an electrolyte imbalance from sweating so much.

The sensations continued on and off through most of December when I did yoga, and I continued to assume that I just needed to watch my fluid levels. Despite loads of water, sea salt, and other electrolytes before and after class, the sensations continued; I began to wonder if something else was happening. The feeling wasn't bad or uncomfortable—it was just *new*. It wasn't like a pain or pleasure that occurred in the body, because this sensation seemed to extend beyond my body into the air around me. I did not know what this vibrating sensation was, and my current belief system had no means of reconciling the new experiences.

In addition to the sensations at the Bikram yoga classes, I started sensing things and having visions that I had never had before with startling accuracy. The visions occurred when I was relaxing or meditating; strong, vivid images would "pop up." My so-called experiences of ESP—extrasensory perception—went from nonexistent to daily occurrences. I knew instinctively when someone was about to call or text me before they did. I thought the coincidences were interesting but didn't give them much thought. Our dietary changes seemed to be clearing out so much gunk; it made sense that we had been bogging some of our abilities down with bad food.

* * *

Over the course of roughly a year, our symptom lists went from extensive to nonexistent. The vast changes in physical health occurred that first year, with the emotional and mental improvements taking place in the following months and years to present day. (For before and after photos of Lance and me, please visit www.equilibriumdiet.com.) The following are symptom lists for both Lance and me taken one year after our first juice fast—our lists are identical, so only one list is provided.

- sleeping six to eight hours a night without a need for a nap
- improved vision
- can feel emotions and energies of ourselves, other people, and animals
- much stronger immune system
- clear thinking
- not easily angered or emotionally altered
- a sense of daily peace and a milder temper
- a positive attitude with limited tolerance for negativity
- rudimentary understanding of which fears are our fears and which are other people's fears

Both Lance and I have severe allergic reactions to all food additives: chemicals, preservatives, colorings, wheat, and pasteurized dairy. Our throats start to swell shut, and sinuses become congested. We take MSM (methylsulfonylmethane) and enzyme supplements on the few occasions we accidentally eat something that sets us off. Roughly two years after our dietary changes, all of our initial health complaints were gone—even seasonal allergies, and we live in the "pollen haven" of South Carolina. I do still have slight dark circles under my eyes from years of adrenal burnout, but these are much improved and improving as my mineral stores are rebuilt. Additionally, neither of our children have ever had an ear infection or infection of any kind; they have never been on an antibiotic or any other OTC or pharmaceutical drug—we are all *healthy*.

CHAPTER 4

The Economist and the Atheist

To understand our tectonic shifts in consciousness that occurred after we began the cleanses and Equilibrium Diet, we should flash back to before July 2010. Back then, I thought I was a perfectly happy, hyper-rational economist; I'd also been an atheist living in the middle of the Bible Belt for all of my adult life. I was emotionless to the outside world, and the closest thing I ever had to a spiritual experience was visiting the Biltmore House in Asheville, North Carolina. Seeing the castle that capitalism had built was awe-inspiring and beyond words in my eyes. I had seen the palaces of Russia and Europe, and to see that something just as grand was built on the principle of the free market instead of serfdom was simply tear jerking.

I had always loved ideas and theories, particularly theoretical math and physics. I did wonder about the possibility of dimensions beyond our third dimension, like the fourth and fifth and sixth dimensions, because mathematically an infinite number of dimensions exist; it seemed illogical to only have three dimensions in our physical reality. I wondered about realms beyond this world, but I did not believe in, or have faith in, anything beyond the physical third dimension. Perhaps that was part of what led me to become an economist. Or perhaps it was because economics fit so naturally into the way my brain already operated—I was constantly looking at ways to improve efficiency in the world around me. I was constantly observing and working with the incentive structure.

As a farmhand in high school in Idaho, I mastered wheat collection from the combines as a bank-out wagon driver. I would ferry grain from the combines in the field to the trucks, devising systems that would keep the three to five combines moving at all times. So when I sat in my first economics class during my freshman year at Wofford College, it was like having a third party narrate my thoughts for me. Economics seemed to be ingrained in me. Economists are bloodhounds. We are always tracking the scent of the incentive trail. Economists have an uncanny ability to shuffle through all the white noise and see what really matters in any observed outcome—the incentives. We find diamonds in buckets of quartz because we *understand* the rules. Instead of just correlation, we seek *causation*.

I have always been a perfectionist—not in terms of the material world of *stuff* but in terms of ideas and thoughts. I am constantly searching for the truth and the best way to do anything, which circles right around to efficiency. Economics provides simple models to help decipher the truth. Economics applies the laws of physics to people, businesses, and countries. Literally, the mathematical formulas used in physics to prove conservation of matter are used in economics to prove cost minimization and profit maximization. Most of the great advances in economics come when an economist "discovers" a new way to apply an existing law of physics. For me, physics and quantum mechanics were natural extensions of economics. I found all three subjects fascinating and inseparable. This runs contrary to some other scientists. Many scientists would say the two models—standard physics and quantum mechanics—seem to contradict each other. Many competing theories try to unite the subatomic and atomic levels.

Newton's mechanistic view of the world and general physics states that the laws of the universe are fixed and predictable. Physics says that all matter behaves according to predetermined principles and laws like gravity. But Newton *assumed* matter actually existed. Matter can be broken down into smaller and smaller parts. At first the smallest part was an atom, then the parts of atoms like electrons, and then subatomic particles like quarks. Today we aren't sure that any *part* of an atom actually exists; atoms appear to be infinitely divisible—*we are made of stuff that appears to not exist*.

Quantum mechanics describes how these particles and subatomic particles behave. This is the realm where scientists are able to fly particles through brick and metal walls with no explanation. Photons of light appear to be particles and waves at the same time. A separated molecule always retains the information of the whole—as if it were never separated at all. Quantum mechanics describes our universe at the subatomic level that is invisible to the naked eye. Newton's laws lend predictions to the actual physical matter we see. It seems illogical to have two different sets of rules for different-sized particles. In my field, this would be like having two sets of rules for microeconomics and macroeconomics. Economists realize that the macro—the big picture—comes from the micro particles. The macro is the law of weighted averages. Anything an individual micro unit does can be observed at the micro level. It can also be observed at the macro level. You won't see the individual units, but you will see the weighted average results of all the actions.

To me, this implies that *everything* follows the rules of quantum mechanics. Regardless of size, molecules, particles—even you and I—follow the rules of quantum mechanics, and many new experiments in quantum mechanics are illuminating this symmetry of the microscopic and macroscopic. Physicists have proven that particles—clumps of atoms—behave like their subatomic counterparts.

* * *

The Atheist

Never in my entire life before December 2010 would I have considered myself religious. In my youth, before age eighteen, I was agnostic. My mother grew up Presbyterian and forced me to attend Sunday school as a child. Other than an introductory world religions course in college, Sunday school was my only dabble in religion or spirituality.

I hated it. At age ten, I questioned the Sunday school teacher about the logic of God, the devil, and Jesus Christ. I remember saying, "If God is omnificent and omnipotent, then why not simply abolish the devil?"

The Sunday school teacher said, "Because then there wouldn't be any need for faith."

I didn't understand how that answered the question for anyone. I would ask, "If God is all-powerful, then why would he make anyone—Jesus—suffer for the sins of other people when he could just forgive them without any bloodshed?" My Sunday school teacher never answered this or any of my questions. We always needed to "move on" instead.

It would be twenty years later, when I was almost thirty years old, that I finally acknowledged and accepted the amount of power, and rationality, people will give up when faced with fear—fear of illness, fear of hell, fear of death. As a child, I saw religion as a part of culture that was almost 100 percent correlated with geography. The religion prevalent in the part of the world or country where a person was born would most likely form the person's religious or spiritual belief system. In my mind, this did not coexist with the idea of free will. When only one pre-specified group of religious followers go to heaven, free will is not possible if God chooses your geographic location, which then determines your religion.

As I aged, I became more logical, more analytical, and an adamant atheist. There were certain things I knew to be intrinsically flawed, including all major religious texts. The biblical fallacies were just too numerous: Jesus being born of a "virgin," the earth being 5,000–6,000 thousand years old, God preaching love but then eliciting fear through judgment.

When I argued with religious friends and family members, they usually agreed with me about the flawed biblical logic but would always fall back on what I saw as their "safe" routines and thought patterns. I did not understand how people could claim to interpret an almost 2,000-year-old text literally but then throw out the parts where rape was okay and women were property. Once you don't interpret *everything* in the Bible literally, then you are picking and choosing what you do interpret. At that point, you are making up your own rules and beliefs as you go along. Religion becomes arbitrary, with the decisions being made by whoever is in charge. Once I pointed this out, the opposing arguer would always leave the room or tell me I was going to hell. I didn't like how churches and religions told people how to live their lives; I didn't like the judgment of others, the guilt, and the shame. In general, I did not like being told what to do by *anyone*.

CHAPTER 5

Outliers

Outliers are observations that fall a long way from the average. If the average height for men is five feet eight inches, and we see a man who is seven feet tall, the seven-foot-tall man is an outlier. Prior to my dietary changes, I knew of two outliers that strayed from my atheist view of the world; the first involved affirmations, and the second, past-life regression. Some of the time, scientists and economists toss outliers out of their datasets or give them less weight relative to other more "normal" observations. The reasoning is that those outliers are probably being observed because of measurement error either on the subject or researcher's part.

Measurement error implies that the seven-foot man's height was incorrectly reported or inputted in some way. The outliers are considered to be faulty data. But what if the seven-foot man was measured *correctly*? In the absence of measurement error, outliers provide additional information. As a probabilistic atheist, I viewed other people's supposed "spiritual" experiences as outliers—I assumed they were due to faulty reporting. I had never seen or experienced anything spiritual; therefore, I drastically discounted the value of others' experiences. I didn't know the other inputs in the situation. I wondered, "Did people not have their glasses on? Were they dreaming? Were they on drugs or alcohol? How much exaggeration do they typically use when speaking?"

However, if a seven-foot-tall man exists—which today we know is true—measurement error in our height example is zero.

When measurement error is zero, that means that the outlying observations are accurate representations of reality. I want to emphasize this again: when observations are correctly measured, the data reflect reality. The observations may be on the fringe and outside the normal range, but the data point is legitimate. In these cases, the outliers contain tremendous amounts of information. They are not "normal," but they provide specific information—in this case, the data say, "Humans can be much taller than five feet eight inches." (Or in the case of spiritual experiences, "Humans can feel, see, and hear much more than just their five senses permit.") Then we can look at identifying what *makes* the observations *not* normal. What other variables helped create this incredibly tall man? The outliers can be used to rethink our models of how we approach a problem, our thought patterns, or the world.

Outlier #1: Positive Affirmations on Athletic Performance

I had two experiences that led me to believe the mind could directly influence the physical body. The first occurred in college when one of the athletic trainers was completing his senior thesis on the effects of affirmations on athletic performance. He used volleyball players' vertical jump measurements before and after they said ten positive statements and ten negative statements. We, the volleyball player subjects, were not told the point of the study at the time. At the time, I thought it was all a bunch of mumbo-jumbo, but, interestingly, my results were the most dramatic on the team. After the positive affirmations, I had my normal vertical, but after repeating the negative statements, my vertical dropped three to four inches (depending on the trial). That decline has always remained in my memory. Other than blaming luck or a small sample size, my model of the world could not explain the results. Today, years later, I have seen many of the studies linking positive thinking and affirmations with performance, both athletic and nonathletic. Each study reports the same results my vertical jump yielded—*thoughts affect performance.*

Outlier #2: Past-Life Regression

The second outlier I had observed was regression therapy. Regression therapy is a technique used by psychologists to self-hypnotize patients to access portions of their memory that have been disjointed, or cut off, from the conscious brain. The severance usually occurred because of a trauma or fear the patient experienced in the past. Regression therapy can be used for mental and physical illnesses stemming from childhood or before—even in utero and past or parallel lives. Though I was an avowed atheist, the data I read on past lives was intriguing. The more I researched studies on past lives and saw the collected data and experiences, the less and less I viewed the data as simple measurement error. I began to think that maybe these data were true outliers, and maybe we could learn from them.

Researchers have collected a lot of evidence to suggest that many of us may have been here (or other places) before our current time and space. Researchers Carol Bowman, Ian Stevenson, Jim Tucker, and Tom Shroder have documented over four thousand cases around the world of past lives being accurately described by children.[1] Often the children can speak in languages they have never been exposed to in this life and can correctly identify past-life relatives, locations, and special events.

Bowman identifies her past-life stories by looking for children who recount the past lifetime in a matter-of-fact tone, consistently over time, and possess knowledge beyond their experience, as well as corresponding behavior and traits.[2] Her interest in past-life regression peaked when her five-year-old son sat on her lap in a hypnotherapy session and described himself as a terrified solider fighting a Civil War battle. Bowman had no knowledge of her son ever being exposed to Civil War history, and certainly not Civil War specifics.[3]

In clinical psychology, regression therapy is often used to access information in the subconscious mind. Many psychologists use regression therapy to delve into the subconscious fears and memories of their clients. Along the way, some psychologists apparently stumble upon past-life information as well. Perhaps the most well-known psychiatrist to stumble into past lives with patients is Brian Weiss. In all of his books, Dr. Weiss documents the regression therapy sessions of his clients and the past lives that they describe.[4] Interestingly, even though Brian's clients under hypnosis relay very detailed past-life information, many of them do not remember anything when they come out of hypnosis. Weiss explains that this is a protection mechanism of the conscious mind and ego. Hypnosis experiences will not be consciously remembered if the information conflicts with the patient's beliefs and thought patterns in this lifetime. For instance, people who are very religious and believe in only one lifetime are unlikely to recall past lives consciously, because it conflicts with their current belief system. Only those open to the possibility of other lifetimes will be able to consciously remember the session.

This could also explain why the vast majority of children's past-life documentation occurs in Eastern societies, which are more accepting of a belief in reincarnation. Western children would have already chosen a "protective" conscious or unconscious block to that information. This helps them fit in to their world and family as best they can. This blocking or splitting of the mind would be more likely to occur the less a culture embraces the right brain, which does not involve logical thinking.

These two very different sets of outliers would provide my conscious brain with the foundation for possibility in the years to come. The possibility that there may be more to this world—and to humans—than science, and I, initially believed.

CHAPTER 6

Accidental Enlightenment

I was an investment-banking analyst, I've been deposed as an expert witness by some of the toughest lawyers in the country, and I'm a PhD economist, but nothing prepared me for the night of December 26, 2010. That was the night my model of the world, the illusion I lived in, shattered forever.

I was an atheist. In my atheist view of the world, people did not have instincts or feel energies or emotions, or talk to God and have him talk back. I did not know or believe anything other than the material physical world. At 3:00 a.m. on December 26, 2010, the shell that kept me from the energetic world—our instincts and the world of vibrations—cracked wide open. In an instant, I went from a scared atheist to a confused spiritualist. Over the next several months, I would gradually put words to the information and feelings I received that horrible, wonderful night.

* * *

Lance and I were at his parents' house in Lancaster, South Carolina, to spend the holiday with family. The food had been a bit difficult for us to maneuver. We had no desire to eat the normal Christmas treats we had scarfed down in years past, and family dinners can be tough when you avoid meat at night and all sugar, preservatives, and processed food. We ended up bringing and cooking most of our own food—some family members were more supportive of this than others.

When all of the Christmas festivities were over and the night came to a close, we all headed off to sleep uneventfully. I slept soundly until around 3:00

a.m. when I awoke quickly in a state of sheer terror. I was having a dream that bad energies were trying to enter my body. I had dreamed about ghostlike energies before that chased me in my childhood dreams, but I had never dreamt of one physically trying to get into, or press into, my body.

These were bad energies. They did not feel warm and loving; they were dense and oppressive, the opposite of anything you would want to be cuddling up with on a winter night. I could not see, hear, smell, or taste them in my dream; I could only feel something thick and dense trying to push into the front of my body. It was like being pinned down by a grid of energy and not being able to move. It was not that I was being electrocuted or shocked; it was a firm, invisible pressure holding me down.

It was a frightening dream. Even more terrifying was that when I woke up, the oppressive energy was still there. I continued to feel a blanket of dense energy pressing down on me. It felt like aggressive little spider webs all around me. The energy or spirit was trying to get into my body. It wasn't shoving me out; it was just trying to get in with me. I knew it wasn't good and that I didn't want it there. I didn't know how to fight it. I couldn't see anything, yet it was very intense.

I did not know what was happening, and I was very afraid. I was culturally Christian because I grew up in the United States in a nondenominational Christian church, so I really only had Christian theology to reference. The first thing that came to my mind was possession—demons or evil spirits were trying to enter my body.

I physically could not sit up in the bed to run away, and then instinctively, I understood that even if I could run, it would not help me. The only thing I could think to do was pray. I had not prayed in decades. I was an atheist. Atheists don't pray. I did not know how to pray. But I tried. It was the only thing I could think to do, given I couldn't move and I couldn't scream. I started praying over and over again. I tried to say the Lord's Prayer, because I had seen in some Hollywood movie that a possessed person could not get all the way through the Lord's Prayer. I tried to say the prayer in my mind—I couldn't remember all the words, and I have no idea why; I was stumbling through parts. I was in a state of panic—sheer terror swept over me.

I thought to myself, *Am I possessed? How can I not remember the Lord's Prayer?* I just said it the night before in church at the Christmas Eve service. I said it in Sunday school every week as a kid. I had never forgotten it at the countless weddings and funerals and Christmas services I had attended in my life. Fear engulfed me. Tears were streaming down my face. I kept trying and trying to complete the Lord's Prayer, but I could not complete it.

And then I stopped—I could not remember it on my own. And then, for the first time in my life—I started *really* praying. This was beyond some memorized prayer or scripture. I started asking for help. I started praying because it was all I could think to do, and I prayed to the god I was most familiar with from my youth: "God, Jesus, I have never believed in you before. I don't know what this horrible energy or entity is, but if you exist, please help me. This battle is beyond my physical abilities."

I did this intensely and fearfully for several minutes, repeating the words over and over with no relief. I may have even thought something like, *If you help me out here, I'll look into you (God) later.* But the dense and scary energy was still there pushing down on me.

And then, for some reason, I tried to say the Lord's Prayer again. I had my eyes closed. The oppressive spider webs were still pressing down on me, and I still could not move or scream. This time I made it all the way through the prayer without a mistake ... and this time, I was not alone. Suddenly, it was as if lightning had struck. A booming male voice chimed directly in my ear, **"Lead us not into temptation and deliver us from evil. For thine is the kingdom, the power and the glory, forever and ever. Amen."**

Instead of darkness behind my eyes, all of a sudden it was like someone had turned on beautiful, golden, wispy lights. I saw a bright but misty gold and yellow color and the blurry image of a man's head in the center. The man looked like Jesus—he had long brown hair and was about thirty years old; he could have played Jesus in any movie or television show. There was no questioning whether or not this male voice actually spoke; it was so loud and powerful that there was no guessing what had been said. I did not have to strain to hear anything—the words vibrated through my entire being. In that instant, the scary energies evaporated—golden light shot into me and moved all around me. It was as if someone had plugged me into a light socket of golden spiritual energy that shot from my toes through my head. It was like being a stationary lightning bolt.

The energy rushed into and around my body. It charged me with love, peace, inspiration, and information. The sensation was timeless; I had no sense of time. It was as if time evaporated into some man-made theory or construct. I was there forever and in an instant, all at once. I felt very much at peace, more at peace than I had ever felt in my life; it was extreme serenity. It was a feeling of heaven on earth. The entire universe seemed to make sense to me; everything fell into place, and I realized—*knew*—that I was literally love, and that I was always connected to the Divine, and that I channeled Divine energy.

I also felt extreme forgiveness and compassion for all living beings. I felt connected to everything and everyone. The boundaries of our world simply slid away—or I was lifted beyond them. I saw that in the next realm, the illusion of the third dimension—Earth—subsides, and we are all connected. *We are all one.*

The energy I felt, this golden and heavenly sensation, this was all of us. It was our truth. The truth of all life everywhere, in all time and space. It was a feeling of absolute power, forgiveness, and love. The golden glowing light was everywhere inside me and all around me. No more words were spoken; wisdom was simply experienced. The concepts, the knowing, were suddenly there inside of me. I felt them and knew them to be true at a level beyond our physical world. It was as if a mega computer had instantly downloaded emotions, truths, and sensations to me. This information was not from planet Earth. It was not of this dimension. It was more—*much* more.

This is what I *knew*:

1. God is within each one of us. God is all-encompassing and beyond human words and understanding. God is acceptance and the lack of all resistance of all things.
2. Everything is connected, within us and around us. Love and peace are at the heart of our true nature and what we are here to express and remember.
3. Time and space are relative and help explain our dimension but not necessarily other dimensions.
4. We come to this world for a journey, and we know individually why we are here. To find our journey, we must remember our true selves.
5. We have more than five senses. We have the ability to access much more information than we have restricted ourselves to observing in the physical dimension. These are our long-forgotten instincts. When we return to physical health and a natural state of balance, we awaken the senses that people on this planet call both "instinct" and "psychic ability." Those two words are synonymous—two terms for the same thing.

My experience was beyond this physical world, and I am hard-pressed to accurately or adequately describe it using mere three-dimensional vocabulary. I still struggle to find the words. The experience was not from here. It cannot be spoken. Describing the enlightenment experience is like trying to describe feelings or emotions; there is only so much you can say to relay an emotion. Emotions must be *experienced*; they are *felt*. It is a connection of simply knowing, because it resonates within you and all around you.

Just as suddenly as it began, the download stopped. The man's face disappeared. My body still buzzed and radiated the unconditional love from Jesus and the Divine. I was still a bit frightened but overall much more at peace and relaxed. I woke Lance up, and I was speechless. I cried for a few minutes. Lance thought I was dreaming and crazy, but he tried to calm me down. I didn't sleep the rest of the night; I lay there and thought about what had happened and how different I felt—almost transformed. Instead of energies pressing in on me, now I felt like I was buzzing. There was an electric field around me. It didn't hurt; it was just there, like a blanket of bliss all around me. I felt like I was floating or hovering near the bed instead of lying on it. The next day, my skin teemed with the sensation, and I was more at peace than I had ever been. The vibrations of my body continued to hum for days. I had experienced a direct connection to the Divine. It was a token of remembrance of who I really was.

* * *

If someone had asked me what enlightenment was five years ago, I probably would have described a physical feeling of bliss and an understanding of the big picture of the universe. I would have assumed that some higher being or god would have explained all of this knowledge to the enlightened one. All of my descriptions would have been very ordinary and three-dimensional. My definition would not have been special in any way. I used to think the enlightened were just very wise and comfortable with themselves. I thought it was a three-dimensional intelligence—an intelligence still of this earth.

The charged feeling, the blanket of vibration was familiar—it was the same feeling I had been trying to escape from in hot yoga but on a much greater scale. I had just experienced a transcended state far greater than any meditation had ever taken me, but my mental self—my ego—was struggling to integrate what had happened.

My knowledge of the universe changed in an instant, and I went from atheist to knowing—*I knew.* I understood. My rational, atheist thought forms did not believe in such events or experiences. What had just happened? What did it mean? My atheist beliefs evaporated. How did this information I had been given mesh with the material world? With spirituality? With science? With me? Who or *what* was I?

CHAPTER 7

Atonement

I was on Christmas break from Clemson. I was supposed to be studying for school. I was supposed to be working on my dissertation. I wasn't doing any of that. I spent my days in a trance-like state, partially in awe and totally confused. Then night would come. The vibrations would get more intense, and I would feel afraid again. I couldn't sleep. I was too scared, too awestruck, and too confused to sleep.

I Googled *vibrations, energy, possession,* and *spirit encounters* for hours on end during my insomnia. Nothing I found helped me. Some of it made me more afraid. Other parts were kooky. Nothing explained what I had just experienced. My cycle of confusion continued until it was time to return to school. I was exhausted. I knew I couldn't function at school in my current zombie-like state. I had to make a decision on what to do. What do you do when reality shatters in an instant and no one else knows? The world around me continued unchanged, but I knew the physical world was an illusion, a shadow of some greater truth. I couldn't tell people. What good would it do? Shatter the illusion for them too? More than likely, they would just think I was crazy.

No—experiences like the one I had just didn't happen in the world. So I did the only thing I knew how to do—I denied it. I told myself it was a great experience, but it didn't matter. It didn't matter to anyone, and it didn't matter to me. I had to function in the unchanged world around me, and this world didn't include enlightenment, energies, or spirituality. I could always remember the experience and that state of bliss. I could go back there in my mind to visit, to dream. But that was it. It was my secret, and no one else needed to know that I had seen beyond this world.

I hadn't told anyone but Lance, and even he didn't know much. I didn't want to worry him either. He was supportive. He knew me as the lady who could not lie—not even a white lie—so even if he didn't want the story to be true, he knew it was. I could tell his concern was mounting as he watched me withdrawing and not sleeping, which was not my normal outgoing self.

Denial was a good choice. It would keep Lance from worrying. It would keep the world at bay. With the start of school, I tried to force myself to let it be, to stop thinking about my experience and to get on with my normal routine. I did a pretty good job of it. To the outside world, I seemed functional. I seemed completely normal. I continued to teach my economics classes. I completed all my classwork. I didn't tell a soul about what had happened. I tried not to think about it. The truth was I couldn't stop thinking about it. My memory of the experience created a lot of emotional distress. My atheist reality had been shattered, and I was left reviewing my life with new eyes.

In reviewing my past, I didn't like what I saw. I began to second-guess every decision I had ever made; I began to criticize anything I'd ever done that might have been a mistake. To the outside world, I was fine. But inside, I sank into a depression as I continued to analyze myself and torment myself over decisions I'd made and bridges I'd burned long ago. The one that played over and over in my head was a decision I made in college—to get an abortion. Lance and I were young, and I found out I was pregnant. I was terrified. We were not prepared emotionally, mentally, financially, or spiritually to have children.

I thought about what life would be like if I had a baby, and it did not look good. I couldn't even imagine the resentment that would build between a couple when neither is ready to have a child. I do not remember being all that emotional about the decision. It was fairly emotionless, based entirely on the plan I had set out for my life and the economics of that point in time. I pretty much forgot the incident. I was an atheist, so I did not believe I had done anything other than "family planning." I was fine, and it did not haunt me, at least for a while. It did not haunt me until I started to feel the energies and until I knew there was life after death. Not necessarily in the sense of a heaven but in the case of coming back to learn more and right your past wrongs—like karma.

After I experienced heaven (or enlightenment), I felt the peace, but my analytical mind was still constantly running, and my fear took over. Potential spiritual implications began to weigh on me more heavily. I felt awful; I was so embarrassed, so ashamed; I felt like people were judging me—I was judging myself. I thought to myself, *Oh no, what have I done? I did not believe in anything in college; I believed in death after death, and now I know that is not true. What does this mean for me? I have done the unforgivable. I have killed another person. I have created suffering for another. How could a baby ever forgive me? I can never forgive myself.*

And so the years passed, and I did not forgive myself. I beat myself up over it a lot. I tried not to think about it, but I went through cycles of depression. I tried to stay too busy to think about it. Then somehow I discovered shadow work. Our "shadows" are all those aspects of ourselves that we deny, disown, and shove aside. Shadow work is based on the psychology work of Carl Jung, and it is similar to the Eastern philosophy of mindfulness. Debbie Ford's book *The Dark Side of the Light Seekers* changed my perspective. I was willing to accept that we as humans are all things; we possess the full array of human characteristics rooted in two sources: love and fear.

I began to understand that no one, not even an unconditionally loving god, would ever be able to be meaner to me than I was to myself all those years. I learned that even self-criticism is a form of *protection*. When we tear ourselves down and fill our thoughts with self-loathing, we create a world where no one will ever be meaner to us than we already are to ourselves. The self-criticism builds layer after layer of thought patterns that then create our life. Then one day we look in the mirror, and the criticism is all we see. I had to believe I killed someone I loved to be motivated enough to actually look within myself—instead of plowing through life as a left-brained robot. I had to be in an emotional place of immense darkness and fear to be willing to get out of my brain and look within.

Everything—all of the negative emotions, the self-hate, the self-criticism—was a part of my path. My strong will had to fall. I had to atone for my sins. This was not an atonement to some external power; it was the unconditional acceptance of the self. I had to see and love myself for the terror I experienced as a young woman who subconsciously believed her life would be over if she had a child. I had to learn and know that absolutely everything happens for a reason, and that reason is always in our highest interest, no matter how awful we feel at the time. In fact, sometimes the more awful we feel about an event initially, the more peace we feel when we are able to look back at it and view it as a gift. Embracing myself meant that I stopped fighting against the current of my life—I began to relax and tried to flow wherever my river took me.

CHAPTER 8

Mission Control

Three months had passed since my accidental download from the Universe, but I still had no plans of sharing my experience with *anyone*. In my spare time, I continued my fervent research on natural healing and nutrition. Lance and I began heavily detoxing again with liver flushes and heavy metal cleanses; we had been much too aggressive and were struggling to eliminate the toxins as quickly as we were releasing them. I was trying to find the best way of eliminating the painful symptoms. Fatigue, body aches, and brain fog were wearing on both of us. I started to feel like we would never get better. I kept learning. I kept searching, but I grew weary. After months of physical and emotional pain, depression began to trickle in. It had been a long journey. Probably too long, and I was on the verge of quitting.

It was then that somehow, magically, I found Robyn. Robyn was a hands-on touch kinesiologist. If you Google that, it won't pop up. I didn't know what a hands-on kinesiologist was; I didn't know what energy work was. I learned that a hands-on kinesiologist uses part massage, part manual adjustment, and part energy stimulation to align the body, mind, and spirit. I would later learn that it is a lot like Network Chiropractics, founded by Donny Epstein, which is a form of chiropractic care that does not "crack" people but instead shows the brain where stagnant energy is residing in the body to allow the brain to go access the energy.

Robyn was a mother of five children and worked out of her home. She helped to align people skeletally, muscularly, and energetically. She wasn't listed in the phone book or on the Internet. She didn't have business cards. Somehow, I don't remember how, I was given her number to call. Robyn was a Christian. I don't know if she believed in psychics. I don't know if she knew about what I now call instincts. Regardless, she introduced me to the energy world in a way that helped free me of my fear. She didn't intentionally teach me about the subtle energy world—there were no lessons per se. I don't know what Robyn felt or sensed during our sessions together, but I do know that while she worked, she was working on something much deeper, much more subtle than my physical body.

Each session with Robyn was very relaxing and emotional. The energies around my body would somehow come alive beneath her hands. The vibrations from hot yoga and enlightenment were back, but this time the experience for me seemed more controlled—and, for the first time, I wasn't alone. Regardless of what Robyn could or could not sense, it gave me peace knowing that she worked calmly, regardless of my emotional state and the vibrations that would surface. She took everything in stride, like it wasn't a big deal. Love, hate, regret, stress—it didn't matter because each serves a purpose. Maybe these vibrations were not the big, scary deal that I had been making them into so far. I began to see the body as energy, as an extension of the soul. This was the beginning of acceptance—acceptance that I was more than just a physical body. Acceptance that I was energy and a spiritual being. Acceptance that I had seen the truth about humanity the prior December in those early morning hours. I still wasn't going to tell anyone about it. What would be the point? But it became "okay" in my mind that it happened. Instead of seeing enlightenment as a scary shove into the vibrational world, I began to accept it as a gift. For the first time, I began to feel grateful.

* * *

Just because you've been given a gift doesn't mean you want to share it with the world. I had no intention of telling anyone about my experience or the vibrations I was starting to feel. My plan was to finish my PhD, become an economist, and teach at the college level. I thought I was here to teach incentives and supply and demand—I was wrong. The Universe had other plans for me. Exactly one year after Lance and I began our dietary changes, I was given a message.

I was on vacation in Priest Lake, Idaho, in August 2011. I had begun meditating in June to alleviate my chronic neck and shoulder pains—the pains were probably the result of hours at a computer screen and years of intense volleyball training. In the lake house bedroom, I lay down to meditate for a few minutes. I performed my routine of relaxing all of my different body parts. I began focusing on my breathing. All of a sudden, the lake house and bed were gone. I was somewhere else. I was in a beautiful, quiet white place. It was neither inside nor outside. I was in a place where there was no inside or outside. I felt unconditional love and support. I felt extreme strength and infinite loving power. I was being cradled by two beings of light. One was entirely white, and the other was electric blue. They looked like different parts of a candle flame. They were beautiful. I felt their loving vibrations moving like waves all around me. And then they spoke to me.

They said, "We are going to tell you why you are here. You are here to connect the two sides of the brain: the left side and the right side—science and spirituality. You are going to write a book, and you are going to call it, *Atheist to Enlightened in 90 Days*."

While I was with them, everything was so peaceful, so natural. There was no such thing as confusion or lying. I didn't ask questions because everything made perfect sense. I was mesmerized by their presence. I just wanted to stay there with them. They were magnetic—they were *home*.

Just as quickly as I'd arrived, I was gone. In a flash, I was lying in the bed again with my eyes open. It was as if a time warp had occurred and I switched dimensions momentarily. When I got back, no time had passed at all. It was as if I was about to start my mediation all over again. The beings of light were so amazing, so out of this world, so "far out" that I knew I did not fantasize it. There was no change in time to have imagined the beings of light—there was no change in time to imagine *anything*.

A bit dumbfounded, I thought, *Hmmm, that was interesting. Connecting science and religion? You want me to do what? Have you been to Earth and checked this place out? Did you get the wrong planet? Those two categories don't usually go together. Who signed me up for that mission? Wait a minute, are you sure you were talking to the correct human? This can't be right. I'm an academic—academics don't write about enlightenment. I am not enlightened. People will think I've lost it completely.* I was awestruck; the message was so compelling, but I did not understand it or see what it had to do with me. "What does *atheist to enlightened* even mean?" I wondered. I did not know what to do with the information. I certainly wasn't going to go around telling people about it, but I found a napkin on the bedside table and scribbled the message down.

"We are going to tell you why you are here. You are here to connect the two sides of the brain: the left side and the right side—science and spirituality. You are going to write a book, and you are going to call it, *Atheist to Enlightened in 90 Days."*

I immediately showed the napkin to Lance. "That's an awesome title. What does it mean?" he said.

"I have no idea," I replied.

Several weeks later, I found out I was pregnant, and I became too preoccupied with pregnancy to give the Universe's book request much attention.

* * *

Although I did not know what to do with the message initially, it would serve as a beacon over the next several years—a ray of light that grew more and more intense as time marched on. It took time to understand. It took even more time to accept. Actually, it took several years to just break down and give up fighting what I was apparently supposed to be doing. The message was an unquestionable and haunting reminder of what I was apparently here on Earth to do—I had come here to complete a mission, and I would not be able to live in harmony until I accepted that mission.

CHAPTER 9

Coalescence: Human Lie Detectors

Fact: Senecio and violet are two plants with leaves that look virtually identical, with the exception of the very tip of the leaf. Violet leaves come to a point, whereas senecio is slightly rounded. Senecio is toxic. Violet is nourishing and a lymphatic cleanser. The two plants often grow side by side, yet grazing sheep somehow manage to eat only the violet leaves. Sheep know which plants are edible and inedible—sheep have instincts. Have you ever wondered why animals have instincts, but humans are the only species on the planet without the same abilities?

How can a horse sense a storm coming? How can a salmon swim thousands of miles upstream to its exact birthplace? How do birds know the precise day to begin flying south for the winter to avoid getting stuck in uninhabitable conditions? How is it possible that animals know exactly what plants to eat, but humans lack all of these instinctual skills?

Easy. Humans don't lack anything—we *have* instincts.

* * *

Just because you know why you are here on earth does not mean you have to like it. I ignored the message from the beings of light for a long time. I was too busy to listen. Really, I was too afraid. I never doubted for a second that any of my strange experiences were real. Each was more real than anything else in my life. They resonated with me in a way that only true passion, or true calling, can evoke. But I wasn't ready yet—I still had much to learn and many fears to face.

With the birth of my daughter, I began to accept my instincts and the world of energy more and more. I now had a direct connection to the little baby that I had grown. I did not understand the true power of the connection until I started to observe my body in relationship to Genevieve's body. One day in October 2012, Genevieve was sent home from daycare with a cold. At the same time, Lance and I were both experiencing sinus pain and congestion—we thought we were coming down with the virus too. When we arrived home, we gave Genevieve her homeopathic tablets. Homeopathic tablets are a holistic remedy based on the principle that "like cures like." They are like an oral, natural, noninvasive vaccination pellet that works on the energetic body as well as the physical body. Within ten minutes, Genevieve was back to her normal happy self. Oddly, both my symptoms and Lance's were *gone*—all three of us were fine. It was as if Lance and I had taken the homeopathic remedies ourselves—but we hadn't. We had not taken any remedies or had anything to eat or drink.

I pointed out these energetic connections, and it piqued Lance's interest; we both started to track our symptoms in relationship to Genevieve. Every three hours, our symptoms would slowly start to return; we would give Genevieve another round of homeopathic tablets, and within fifteen minutes, all three of us would be back to normal. This was not the first time I noticed feeling what Genevieve was feeling. When she had the German measles (rubella), I had slightly swollen glands and lymph nodes and a rash as well. I assumed that I had rubella too. But then when Genevieve took her homeopathic tablets, my symptoms disappeared just as hers did. Once I noticed the connection, I realized that every pain Genevieve experienced, I experienced too—I was literally *feeling* her pain and symptoms. She was too little to verbally communicate, but she was able to energetically communicate with me.

* * *

Feeling my child's pain seemed natural to me. It reminded me of the instincts many animals have. From an evolutionary perspective, being able to feel your child's pain would be very beneficial. Given two gene pools, one where the parents could sense their child's pain, and another pool where parents could not feel their child's pain, the former would have a huge genetic advantage. Mothers who could feel what their children feel would know instantly if something was amiss and could administer the needed remedy. With regards to viruses, when a cold is caught early, the child would always be better off than if the virus were allowed time to fester. This is particularly beneficial for infants and small children who cannot yet fully communicate. From a biological perspective, such feelings and connections would be a fairly primitive form of intelligence rather than "advanced" or even "spiritual," which is how modern society tends to view ESP and the "sixth sense."

This ability to feel Genevieve's or another person's pain continues to this day. For me, the feelings are strongest with touch; if I touch Genevieve *and* focus on how she feels, it is as if I become her energy field, and I know exactly what she is experiencing. We are all like clouds floating around, and when two clouds get close to each other, the two energies begin to intermix. This is a gradual process, and the feelings sort of float in, and then when I leave the other person's cloud, the feelings of her field float away. I can literally experience and then stop experiencing the symptoms (energy) of an illness just by holding Genevieve and then putting her down and walking into another room.

I could do this over and over again and replicate the feelings. I can feel how an herb or a remedy will make her feel, and I use this ability to find the remedies that make all of the symptoms fade away. I can also feel exactly when she starts to feel better in the same way. This vibrational information can be interpreted by anyone; some people are more in tune than others, but that "energy field" is always there. When people do muscle testing, dowsing, tarot, or rune readings, they are tuning in to that energetic field around the body. "Reading" or "feeling" a person's energy field is one of our primitive instincts.

This energetic field lets us know when we find our own truth; it helps us find our path, just like fish sense how to swim upstream to the exact location where they were born. The lower vibrations, the "dark clouds," are sensed in advance for protection; the fish who listen to their instincts and swim away are the ones who survive to procreate. For us, this means staying away from the person who gives us the heebie-jeebies, or taking the long way to work just because all of a sudden it "feels right." Our right brain, where instincts reside, knows when something is true or false—this instinct is there to protect us from entering into a dangerous situation, eating the wrong plants, or hanging out with the "wrong" crowd.

Because we are made of energy and our thought forms are a form of energy, anything we think will resonate with the body, and each thought will either bring the vibration of the body up (toward those higher dimensions) or bring the vibration down (more toward the third dimension). When a low vibrational energy is introduced to the body, it can literally bring the vibration of the body to a stop—this feels like a mild electrical current in your body suddenly shuts off. To apply vibrational energy in nutritional counseling, I simply sit quietly with an idea and see how it resonates in my body.

1. I sit quietly and notice all of the sensations in my body. I take several deep breaths and focus on inhaling for ten counts and exhaling for ten counts.
2. Next, I see what my truth feels like. I say to myself or out loud, "My name is Katie." I notice the sensations in my body. It feels light, airy, freeing, and good. This feeling is my baseline truth.
3. Then, I notice what an untruth feels like. I say to myself, "My name is Sam." I notice the sensations. I feel dense, sinking, sore, heavy, and constriction in my larynx. This feeling is my baseline lie.

Our bodies know the difference. The more we practice this, the more body awareness we generate, and the faster we notice how our bodies respond. Then we can begin to notice the subtle changes in other people when they are giving and receiving information as well. The more truth you tell, to yourself and others, the higher you raise your vibration and the better you feel. The less truth you tell, the deeper into the third dimension you fall, causing you to feel heavy and tired. This is why we are exhausted when we are not following our true path—we are expending massive amounts of energy trying to deceive ourselves and the world around us. When we align ourselves with our path, we are operating efficiently; we are using all of our valuable energy toward our highest and best interest—fulfilling our true life goals and passions.

* * *

Human instincts are not as foreign to us as we may initially think—sympathy pains are a well-known example. Sympathy pains are well documented in the parenting and baby book literature[1] with to-be dads feeling milder versions of the woman's morning sickness, fatigue, headaches, bloating, and irritability. Major hormonal shifts occur throughout a woman's pregnancy—husbands are simply sensing the changes. Though our perceptions are rarely conscious, we still feel the effects. All of us have the innate ability to "feel energy" or "feel hormones." Perhaps it comes through most strongly during pregnancy, because the hormones are more powerful then, and/or because pregnancy is a more socially acceptable time to allow and feel instinctual. Hormones are energy, and if we are receptive, we can feel these subtle energies. Feeling your child's pain or a pregnant woman's hormones is part of our innate knowledge, instincts we are born with that give us advantages in the world; these are the same instincts that allow animals to sense a storm coming, or salmon to navigate back to their birthplace over thousands of miles of ocean. Animals do not learn these things; no one teaches them—they simply follow the energy patterns in front of them.

I discovered that I was not the first person to attribute the motherly sixth sense to evolution. Joseph Chilton Pearce came to the same conclusion and cited studies on primitive African tribes and mother-infant "bonding."[2] The African women wore their babies on their fronts and backs without any form of diaper and instinctively knew in advance when their babies—from newborns to toddlers—were going to defecate; they would simply take them to the bushes and hold them over the brush.

When asked by researchers how the women *knew* when their babies were going to defecate, the women were puzzled and said something like, "How do you know when *you* have to go?" The women simply sensed the urge in themselves. This ability is present in all of us, and these women had never encountered the Western belief system or processed food to block that primitive knowledge. Pearce calls this "bonding," and it is the same sense that I described earlier. In my opinion, this is the phenomenon that modern "attachment parenting" theories attempt to mimic.

Additionally, the Amazonian shamans who perform ayahuasca tea ceremonies in Ecuador and Brazil claim to be sensitive to energies. Ayahuasca tea is a mild hallucinogenic made from many different herbs but primarily two vines native to South America. It seems that ayahuasca lifts the veil between the conscious and subconscious mind. For drinkers of the tea, this brings them face-to-face with their shadow (the repressed aspects of the self) and their subconscious; the result may be pleasant or unpleasant, because ayahuasca brings the drinker face-to-face with his own fears.

The interesting aspect about ayahuasca is how it is prepared—the shamans prepare the tea differently depending on the participants in the ceremony. Shamans say that they listen to the plant spirits, who tell them which people need which combinations of herbs in the tea. (It can be made from over one hundred different herbs.) The plant spirits also tell the shamans how much of the tea individual participants need to drink in order to have the best opportunity to heal. The shamans, like the African mothers, are tapping into the energy fields of the participants and the plants. They "know" how the herbal combination will affect each individual. The shamans create a tea that perfectly unveils the shadow energies of the drinker. We all can access similar vibrational information—after all, it's our instincts. We just have to remember how to use them. Luckily, this happens naturally as we emerge from nutritional bankruptcy (insolvency) and establish *nutritional solvency.*

* * *

Physical Health

When we are unhealthy, the energy does not flow easily between the different dimensions, and the dense energy moves into the body and weighs down our conscious awareness to only the physical third dimension. When we are "sick," we are too bogged down to experience anything beyond the physical dimension. We may deny the existence of energy and other realms, but that does not mean the realms aren't there; it just means we have closed the veil. The equivalent is like denying the existence of the second dimension (your literal shadow) when the sun goes behind a cloud. The second dimension still exists—you have simply lost the ability to see it and communicate with it. Even though we cannot see the second dimension when the sun is blocked, we are still controlling it. Our physical bodies are the shadow of the next dimension—the fourth dimension. Higher dimensions always funnel down into the lower dimensions. Any movement or change in the third dimension automatically affects and changes the second dimension—our shadow from the sun—even if we cannot observe it because we are in the dark. This is true for everything, including health and healing.

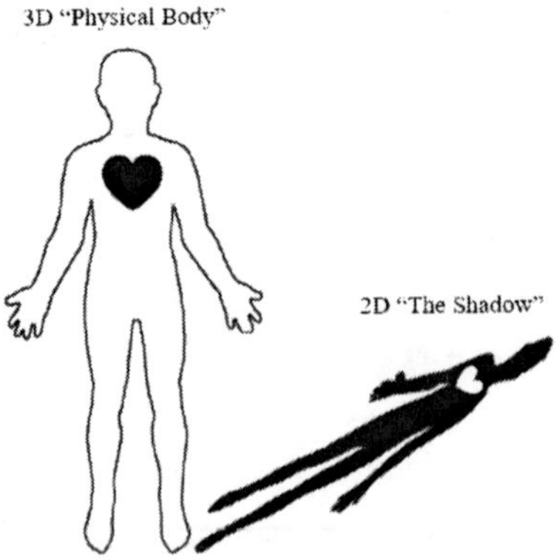

In regard to modern medicine, modern medicine acts only on the physical body—the level of the symptoms. Albert Einstein once said, "Problems cannot be solved at the same level of awareness that created them." Any symptom in the lower dimensions, like the physical body, is not caused in the body; the true roots of the problem will always reside in a higher dimension.

Modern medicine is applied in the third dimension (to the body), but if the cause of the problem resides in a higher dimension—emotions and thought forms—then modern medicine will never truly heal; it will simply mask symptoms. Let's think of modern medicine applied in the second dimension to see the problem.

Think about seeing your shadow again on a sunny day; better yet, suppose you *are* your shadow and live in the world of *only* the *second* dimension. This time, when you look at yourself, you see a hole over where your 2-D heart would be. *Oh dear! That is not good*, you think to yourself. *I must go to a doctor to patch the hole in my heart.* So you go to a doctor of Western medicine, and the doctor looks at your shadow and says, "Yes, my goodness, there is a hole where your 2-D heart should be. Not to worry though; we have a great new technology where we create a thin layer of shadow (the material of the second dimension), and I will actually be able to stitch the cut-out shadow onto the hole in your heart."

Wonderful, you think. *This doctor will fix me up, and I won't have to worry about walking around with this hole and people seeing the hole in me anymore.*

So you have the doctor do the surgery, and he stitches you back together in the second dimension. At first after the repair, you feel okay, maybe even pretty good, with your newfound sense of confidence that now no one can see your hole. But then you start moving your body around, or the light hits at different angles, and now you see the exact same hole; it's just in a slightly different spot, because the light has moved, and you are now seeing yourself (as a shadow) from a new angle.

"What happened?" you wonder. "Why do I still feel this emptiness?" Then you realize what you as a 2-D shadow are—a reflection of your higher self. You see that the hole in the third dimension, the dimension above you, is causing the gap in the second dimension, because when the light hits that emptiness in the third dimension, it portrays white instead of dark on you in the second dimension. The only way to truly heal is to mend the hole in the higher dimension—in this case, the body in the third dimension. Once the heart of the body is filled in the third dimension, the shadow (the second dimension) will be seamless. But there is absolutely nothing anyone can do in the second dimension to repair the problem, because the problem is occurring in a dimension higher than the symptoms you observe.

Our actual bodies in the third dimension are the derivative of what is occurring in our emotions and thoughts. Modern medicine operates in the third dimension—the body—where the symptoms are occurring instead of in the dimension where the problems actually begin—the energetic dimensions of the body (emotional, mental, and higher realms). Our 3-D body is simply "the shadow" of our fourth-dimensional self, and fifth dimension, etcetera. For people undergoing medical procedures, the energetic shift may be enough to shake them out of their "sleep" and help them realize they need to make major emotional, physical, or spiritual changes in their life. But for those who do not take responsibility for their own lives and health, they continue to blame their "bad luck" on bad doctors, bad genes, or fate. In reality, they keep trying to patch a hole in their shadows that does not really exist.

Diet has a large impact on the body and the body's immune system; however, I see a nutritious diet (or the lack thereof) as another symptom of the higher dimensions. When the emotional and mental energy bodies are out of balance, this can manifest in poor lifestyle choices. Someone with clear emotional and mental bodies will probably make better lifestyle choices and not suffer from disease. "Dis-ease" is driven 100 percent by the higher dimensions—emotions and thoughts. One of the blocking mechanisms is diet. We feel stress, and we eat. We feel fear or pain, and we eat. Food, particularly unhealthy food, diverts the mental angst into the body when it is not handled in the dimension where the angst originally occurs. We observe people with heart disease with very poor diets, but diet is the physical manifestation of emotions and thought forms. What emotions or thoughts are people hiding from in food? Why have people decided that they are not worth the investment of high-quality food? When and why did they decide to neglect themselves? Each and every time our diet consists of nutrient-devoid foods, we neglect ourselves—we neglect our needs, and we fail to care for ourselves.

Our physical bodies and experiences are created by our emotions and thoughts. The physical body heals only when the issues are resolved in the higher dimensions. Awakening to this and my instincts was the most powerful realization of my life—it gave me the unequivocal courage to "just say no" to anything standing between me and a higher vibration—regardless of what society, or family members, or experts said. I knew without question what was good for me and what wasn't.

CHAPTER 10

Trouble in Dreamland

The world had become much simpler for me; after putting some of the puzzle pieces of life together, I began to trust myself. My body became the ultimate source of information. I could know in a fraction of a second which foods, drugs, herbs, and vaccinations were vibration raising or vibration killing, for anyone. I had awakened my human instincts and had learned to interpret the information. I knew I could really help people—and I wanted to help. I remembered the request from the beings of light. Sometimes I thought about it; sometimes I thought about writing everything down, but I was still too afraid to share the information I had accessed.

After all, I had graduated with my PhD and was teaching—I was still, first and foremost, a professor. I couldn't talk about energies or vibrations or enlightenment with anyone because I didn't want to be told I was crazy. I didn't want to have to defend something that I knew to be true. I didn't think most people would understand. How could I talk about everything I had experienced? How could I begin to explain what a long, amazing journey it had been? How could I possibly write a book about it? I was a scientist. I couldn't even begin to imagine what the religious zealots would think; after all, this wasn't a near-death experience. It wasn't like I was clinically dead and then came back. I'd had one enlightenment experience in addition to the message about "my mission"—and a whole lot of other incredible discoveries: I could feel emotions; I could feel imbalances in the body; I could vibrationally know which foods and herbs were good for a person and which drugs and activities were not.

People might think I was lying. But why would someone lie about this? Why would an atheist lie about the unimaginable? Money or power? Control?

I'd never cared about any of those things, but how would someone off the street know that? No, I wouldn't write about it. I couldn't write about it. It was too dangerous. It would be too much of a risk for my academic career. The decision was made—or so I thought.

* * *

Then the dreams came. In actuality, the nightmares came. Night after night, the same dream over and over again. In the dream, I was somewhere; I don't know where—it didn't matter where, but it was always the same.

> Three little men would hurry up to me; they looked like Eastern Indians. One by one, each man would come up so close to me that our chests were virtually touching; each would start poking me directly in the chest, right on my breastbone. Over and over again they poked me. Each would repeatedly say to me, "You broke your contract. You broke your contract. It's been three lifetimes, and you've broken your contract. Hurry. Hurry."
>
> Every night I would reply to them. I would question them. "What do you want me to do?"
>
> To which they would each reply, "You know what you are here to do."
>
> I would say, "What about the money? Tell me about the money. If I do what you say, will I be safe financially?"

In those weeks of dreams, they never answered. I knew what it meant. I knew that I was afraid. I was afraid that writing the book would lead me to leave academia and compromise my family's financial security. I had worked so long and so hard in graduate school, and now these little men just wanted me to risk it all. They seemed to want me to leave it all behind. I was an economist—I was a scientist; I had no knowledge or experience in connecting science and spirituality. I had never written a book before. Yet there I sat with dreams that wouldn't stop, and I was resisting what I had been explicitly told to do.

The dreams continued about every other night, and then one night it changed—I had a new dream.

> I was in a house or a classroom with white walls and a big window to the outside world. I could see the full moon in the window. There were two little Polynesian girls in the room with me. They were young teenagers. They were reading each other's minds and communicating telepathically—they were reading my mind. I asked them, "Why is it that you both can read minds but I cannot?"
>
> They both looked at me sadly and turned their faces to the floor. The older girl replied, "It's because you broke your contract." My heart sank. In the dream, I was so sad because I felt that the two teens were living in harmony. They were so happy; they were so natural and at peace. I knew that we were all supposed to be like them—I wanted to be like them. Somehow I also knew that once my contract was fulfilled, I would return to my natural state—I would feel free. I would be free.

When I woke up in the morning, I knew what I had to do. I had both given up and broken through all at the same time. I spoke out loud to the Universe. "Okay, Universe. You win. I give up. I'm sick of fighting you, and I'm sick of being afraid. I'm sick of the little men poking me in the chest. I'm sick of feeling depressed. You know what? I don't care about money anymore. I realize that I am perfectly happy making herbal remedies in the mountains, and if I need to live off the land, I am perfectly capable of living off the land.

"I trust you. I trust that there is something that I am supposed to do here and that you will take care of me along the way. If that means other people think I'm crazy, so be it. If my message falls on deaf ears, I trust that it is supposed to have happened that way.

"Apparently, this is my path, and I will follow it. I will write the book. If you want me to do this, you are going to have to help me, and I mean explicitly help me, because I don't know how to write a book. I commit to you that I will do my part to get it done." I started compiling our health data and my notes throughout our detox that very day. That night I had a new dream.

> I dreamt that I was driving my car down a country road. It was a joy ride through the rolling hills and countryside. The

> hills were green and lush, and the sun was shining brightly. My daughter sat behind me in her car seat singing.

It was a sign, and I knew it. I realized that it had been the first dream in over seven years where I was peacefully driving a car. Most of my dreams involved me trying to drive a car going the wrong direction down the freeway. To make it more stressful, I was usually trying to drive it from the passenger's side with no one in the driver's seat, and I was trying to steer the car with my mind instead of my hands.

Finally, I seemed to have finally negotiated a truce. I sensed that the peace would remain as long as I upheld my end of the deal. I had to write—I had to start telling people.

* * *

Writing was easier than telling people, so I started writing. I wrote slowly at first, but little by little, every day I began compiling the medical records and the sources that I had discovered throughout the journey. It was summertime. So it was easy to uphold my promise of devoting a little time each day to the Universe's project. Then summer ended, and the fall semester began. I let myself get swept up in the hectic day-to-day job of teaching college courses and organizing our department's core classes. A month into the semester, I realized I had stopped writing. I had not made any new progress on the book since the semester began. *Maybe it is okay*, I thought. *Maybe the book can just be a summer project, and as long as I work on it in my free time, the Universe will leave me alone.* After all, it had been a month, and I had not had any more bad dreams. Nothing bad had happened—yet.

* * *

The month of September came to a close, and I found out I was a month pregnant. I had known that I was pregnant, but I humored Lance and spent the seven dollars on a pregnancy test; it was positive—Lance and I were thrilled. It would be an early June baby. A new energy had joined our family, and I knew it would be a little boy.

Despite the excitement, my mind kept turning to miscarriages and all things that could go wrong. I noticed a distinct rash on my hips and legs.

Nothing had changed, except the pregnancy, and I had never had a rash like this before. I could feel the new life within me, and it felt strong. I felt an immediate connection with this tiny being, yet something felt off. About two weeks later, I had a vision of the tiny baby in my uterus, and the baby was cold. It seemed as if blood flow or nourishment was not making it to the baby for some reason. I tried to ignore the vision, but I was concerned. I had also developed a low-grade fever, spleen pain, and swollen lymph nodes. I assumed it was due to allergy and pollen season, but I was trying to rationalize the signs away even though it had been years since I had any allergy problems.

Then came the dream.

> I dreamt I was in the backyard playing with our daughter; I looked up and saw the ghost of a little baby boy floating by the back fence. The little blue spirit looked at me for a second as if to say farewell. Then he disappeared into a golden ball of light. I knew it was him, I knew it was our baby. I sent him love and told him I loved him, but I was too afraid to go to him. I awoke, and in the same instant, I felt his little energy leave my body and this dimension. He was gone.

A few days later, I saw the blood. I miscarried. With the miscarriage, my spleen pain stopped, and my lymph nodes and body temperature returned to normal. I was sad, upset, disappointed, angry, and tired. I accepted it though; a part of me realized that either I or the baby was not ready yet. I thought, *If the baby's not ready yet, I'm not going to rush him. He'll come when he is ready.*

I wanted to be left completely alone; I did not want to be around anyone. The experience made me long for the ancient times and a red tent to which I could retreat for solitude, rest, and release. In ancient times (before 1000 BC), women in most cultures would retreat to some version of a red tent or "moon lodge" during menstruation. The lodges were only for women and provided them with a place to renew themselves in preparation for the coming month. These spiritual places were where many babies were born, where elders passed on and their bodies were anointed with oils. The tents were a symbol of the circle of life—birth, death, and rebirth.

I let the feelings come and go as they pleased. I experienced each but tried to not hold on to any. To a great extent, I released my desire to know and explain everything. Knowing the destruction my body created was also powerful, and it made me realize that I am, and can be, that energy anytime I choose. Deep within me, I knew this was a catalyst—I knew that I would have to give birth to a book before I would have the energy for another human baby. Little did I know that this would be a lesson in accepting change on many levels—this would mean embracing death in the form of not just miscarriage but in life as I knew it.

* * *

A week and a half later, physically, I had really just recovered from the miscarriage—emotionally, I was drained, but I was beginning to come to terms with my new reality. I awoke at 3:00 a.m. after having a dream of my absolute favorite person—my grandma Aurellia. At one hundred years old, she had suffered from congestive heart failure, but she still lived at home, paid her own bills, and made her own breakfast. She did have a caretaker who helped with some things, but she was still mentally sharp.

> October 22, 2013—I dreamt I drove to Grandma's house and got there right at 9:00 p.m. My cousin and her son had just been there to visit Grandma. She had spent the day with them and had a lovely time, they had just left, and I had missed them. Grandma had just gone to bed, but I wanted to be sure to get to see her so I woke her up, and she came in the kitchen and sat with me while I ate something—she did not want anything to eat.
>
> The kitchen was a yellowish-gold color and was organized and clean. Grandma showed me a path on the floor that my aunt made, and Grandma thought it was such a good idea, and she loved it. I thought, *Ah, Grandma has made peace with my aunt and realizes she loves her and is thankful for her.*
>
> We were kind of chitchatting, but Grandma was so, so tired—she was exhausted. When I had finished eating, she was asleep, so I picked her little body up, carried her into her room, and tucked her into her bed. The area around her bed was a little cluttered, but for some reason, I knew she wanted

> me to put her on one side of the bed because my father was going to sleep with her that night; I had to leave room for him to "come visit." I kissed her goodnight and stroked her head and told her I loved her. I knew she was very tired and was now finally at peace and could rest.

When I woke up in the morning, I knew she was gone. I dreamt that I had literally "laid Grandma" to rest after seeing that her soul was so tired. I called Linda, Grandma's helper, to check on her—she told me Grandma was not awake but that she did have her breakfast ready for her. Then she went to check on Grandma, and she would not wake up. She wasn't breathing—she had died in her sleep.

I drove to Clemson to see Grandma one last time. She had donated her brain to science and would be cremated; the local medical university was coming to get her body. She looked so peaceful, just like she was sleeping—it felt so wrong to let the university take her body. I wanted to rub scented oils all over her out of respect for this body that had carried her for so long.

* * *

Grandma left the third dimension at almost 101. With congestive heart failure, we all knew death was coming, but nothing quite prepares you for the actual loss. I really did not cry for her—she passed away in her sleep exactly like she always wanted. I cried for myself and for humanity for losing a soul that cared so much about the world. I just felt heavy and dark and sad, and my normal logical brain was not functioning. I felt out of my own body, like a cloud floating around wherever the day took me. This was the closest experience with death I had ever had, and it offered perspective—I realized that the small stuff does not matter in the grand scheme of things. We need to conserve our resources for the big battles—the overall energy patterns. Our life can be defined by the energy patterns that we create, whether these are love, hate, acceptance, criticism, truth, deception, or fear—we are constantly choosing who we are.

CHAPTER 11

Mission Possible and Vibrational Nutrition

After my miscarriage and Grandma's death, something snapped in me—it was as if the Universe said, "It's time." I suppose I was ready—I was ready to follow the urgent voice that kept pushing me. For eight weeks, I was awakened each day by some internal alarm at 4:30 a.m. I would write for two hours before starting my day. Every spare moment I had—I wrote.

None of it was good. By any measure, the first five hundred or so pages were horrible, but the words needed to come out. I think it was therapeutic for me to finally release the years of emotion and suffering; those pages were another purge. It was the purge of my history, my story, my biases, and my fear—I purged the old me. And then I was done. I had written everything there was to write about my life up until that point. In eight weeks, I had spilled everything there was to spill about myself—I knew it was awful. I also knew I couldn't write anymore—so I rested; I tried to enjoy life. And I did for a while, but after about two months, I started to feel frustrated—I was getting antsy. I was ready to move on with the task of letting go of my past. I started going through the book and ripping out and deleting all the repetition, all the lectures, all the self-pity—all the crap. Finally, the purge was complete. I was a clean slate, and I was ready to write what needed to be written.

* * *

This time, the story flowed. It still did not come all at once; it came in chunks. Chunk by chunk and chapter by chapter, it came. I still had one hang-up, one thing didn't feel right—I had changed the book title to *Atheist to*

Enlightened in 180 Days, in order to incorporate the full time period from taking anti-parasite herbs in August to enlightenment in December. My left brain was snagged on the detail that it was not exactly ninety days from the beginning of our dietary changes to my first enlightenment experience—it was exactly 137 days, and I had begun feeling energy vibrations about 107 days after our initial dietary changes.

But the new title just didn't resonate. After all, I had been told to write a book and call it *Atheist to Enlightened in 90 Days.* Finally, I told my left brain to get over itself, and I changed the title back to *Atheist to Enlightened in 90 Days.* If the beings of light wanted ninety days, ninety days it would be. That night, I learned why in a beautiful dream of jumping off a cruise ship.

> I literally took the plunge and jumped off a cruise ship into sparkling and glittery bright turquoise water. I was swimming with beautiful dolphins and one in particular—I was stroking his skin, and he was playfully nibbling on my left forearm and hand; he seemed to have the same spirit as my dog, Theodore. The dolphin's eyes were not normal dolphin eyes; they were large and black and looked a bit alien-ish, but inside I could see the universe, and I thought, *That is what constant enlightenment must look like.*
>
> The dolphin pulled me through the sparkling water, past pretty strips of land with palm trees; the sky was bright pinks and oranges and reds. It was much more intense than anything on Earth. Zipping through the water, we moved from the open water down to an underground stream or cave. Here, I was walking and trying to hide from an Indian man. I couldn't get away from him; he kept following me. Finally, I got sick of him, and I confronted him and his negativity. I said, "Listen to me. You are so negative. Stop it! You are killing yourself. You are literally dying inside, and you are worried about criticizing yourself. Be positive, find your positivity, and channel it."
>
> The small man broke down. He said, "Of all the people in here, how did you know I was dying? You are right; I need to stop being negative, but how?" When he spoke, his face

> morphed. His eyes grew larger and dark, almost like the dolphin's, and his skin became wrinkled, like small paper wrinkles, and his nose completely disappeared; there was no hole for it. He looked a bit like a human-alien hybrid—it was as if he had been hiding his true self all this time.
>
> I said, "Negativity is a bad habit like any other bad habit. It's just like being an alcoholic and taking that first drink, only instead of wine, it is one small self-criticism—that small slip leads to a snowball effect, and before you know it, you are walking around with a huge, heavy ball of negativity, and it is draining your life force."
>
> He replied, "Three months. It takes three months to set a new habit."
>
> "Yes," I said. "Ninety days. My book is titled *Atheist to Enlightened in 90 Days*."
>
> The man replied in only a partial question. "Book? You already wrote the book." He was speaking as if the book was done.

I awoke knowing several things: everything that needed to be covered had been covered, and the book was complete. Secondly, I knew why the beings of light were so precise about the title when they told me to write the book. I thought it was because that's how long it took me to experience enlightenment—I was interpreting it too literally. Ninety days is the length of time it takes to set a new pattern. In following the step-by-step instructions, other people may not experience the same timeline of events that I did, but they will have established a new pattern for their life. That new pattern will lead them to enlightenment—the new pattern will lead them to remembering who they really are.

* * *

The book manuscript was complete. I wanted to help people, but I still had much to learn and many fears to overcome. *Vibrational nutrition* was solidified when I realized that I could sense anyone's vibrational alignment and not just my own daughter's. This realization struck me quite literally while waiting in line at Wal-Mart. I had my back to the cash register, and all of a sudden, I felt a pain so intense in my right ovary it made me gasp and stumble for support. At first, I didn't realize what had happened; I had never felt anything like it before. I had no prior experience with ovary pain, and yet I knew exactly what it was. As I grabbed the counter, I saw that an overweight female cashier had walked up to our register, and I instantly knew I was feeling her energy field.

I said a prayer in my head and walked away. Sure enough, as the distance between us grew, the pain faded until it ceased when I was about ten feet from her. I have never felt that pain since, but the experience taught me to pay attention. I began noticing different people's energy fields and imbalances. I began realizing what was "mine" and what was coming from others. Actually using this information in a helpful way began with our nanny and her daughter. They walked into our house one morning, and I felt a wave of sinus congestion energy settle into my awareness. Our nanny told me that her daughter had woken up ill and was wondering if they should be around Genevieve. My nanny was into *all-natural* things like I was and had just begun learning about homeopathic remedies. She knew nothing about my instinctual abilities or past experiences, so I simply went to my homeopathic box and began going through different remedies.

With each remedy I picked up, I thought to myself, *How does the little toddler feel when she takes this remedy?* I went through about eight different remedies and then—poof, instant relief. When I picked up *kali mur,* my sinuses and head cleared, and I felt all the stagnant energy flow away. I gave the remedy to our nanny with instructions to give her daughter one tablet every three hours. My nanny texted me ten minutes later saying that the result was amazing and that her daughter was completely better.

I continued to help my nanny whenever she needed something for herself or her daughter; she never asked me how I knew which remedy would work. The tablets gave brief descriptions on the bottles, so perhaps she assumed I had enough experience with each to know when a particular remedy was warranted. I was happy to not have to struggle to explain how or what I was doing, because I didn't know how I would explain it, and I knew I wouldn't be able to lie.

But the day came when I did have to explain what I could do, and amazingly the explanation just flowed from my lips naturally, as if it had always been there and as if my ability was as simple as eating or breathing. It happened with a new friend who worked at the local food co-op. She had a son a bit younger than Genevieve, and she knew from our visits that we were all-natural raw goat's milk drinkers. Every time I saw her, she would ask me about different herbal remedies, and when I learned her two-year-old son had experienced two ear infections, I knew dairy was the culprit. I told her Lance and Genevieve were severely allergic to cow's milk, that the casein protein is incredibly difficult to digest, and that I had never known of an ear infection to be anything other than dairy-related inflammation.

She asked me how I learned they were allergic to dairy, because she knew we didn't go to medical doctors. I replied that a homeopath could test her son, but then I added that I could do it too. I suppose I did this because I knew that it would be tough for her, a young mom, to pay for a homeopath. She asked me if I would test her son, who was there with her in the back of the store that day. A bit nervously, I said, "Sure, I just need to see him."

She took me to her son. When I touched his back, I asked out loud, "Is pasteurized dairy good for him?" And then I described to his mom what I felt. "I feel his throat constrict and sinus passages congest. No, dairy is not good for him. But raw goat's milk is; that clears up the constriction and congestion."

She responded, "You can feel all of that? How can you do that?"

And the answer just flowed out of me. "Lance and I have detoxed and eaten well for so long that we have rediscovered the human instincts. I am sensitive enough to feel the unconscious responses of the body. I'm sort of a human lie detector test. Just like a lie detector, I can sense the subtle unconscious changes in the body when asked a question or presented with a food, herb, or remedy. If the question is true, the person's electrical system relaxes; if the question is false, his electrical system shorts out or stops in various places; this is what I can feel. The lie detector test would record the stress on paper; I just feel the stress. Your son can most likely feel the stress too, but he's just too young to communicate it."

"Wow, that's so intuitive," she said. "It makes perfect sense. Thank you so much." After telling her, I was amazed I had not thought of putting it that way before. I felt better—it was so natural, so simple, and it did make "so much sense."

Our bodies are human truth detectors—we vibrate and radiate when we are speaking, thinking, and acting in truth. This applies to foods that are good for us, herbs that are good for us, and even activities and thought forms that are good for us. Just as grazing sheep can sense the difference between violet and senecio, I could sense the difference between foods just by looking at them. I had become sensitive enough to feel the subtle unconscious responses of the body—I became a human lie detector. Literally, I could know nothing about a food or supplement, and yet I could *feel* how it would impact my body. Oftentimes the strongest vibrational matches would literally bounce and radiate in my hand or in front of my eyes on a store shelf—I understood how a sheep could look at senecio and violet side by side and *know* the difference.

Vibrational testing is similar to a lie detector test or the muscle response testing (MRT) used by kinesiologists and some chiropractors, and each method yields the same results. A lie detector test electronically detects and measures the subtle responses of the body to questions that are either stressors or nonstressors. MRT is typically performed on another person by applying pressure to different body parts in various alignments. Vibrational testing is felt within the body of the questioner; this is the instinct, whereas MRT is isolating the response of the instinct. Metaphysics would call a vibrational tester an "empath," someone who can feel another person's emotions or energy field. Our instincts, which exist to protect us, also allow us to sense subtle shifts in other people and animals. When we are open to bodily communications, we sense truth as connection or increasing and stronger vibrations—we sense untruths as heaviness, deadening, or feeling "cut off."

Vibrational nutrition uses vibrational testing to sense how a food, herb, or pharmaceutical will impact the body. Just like any other lie detector test, vibrational testing works best when the person using her instincts is not biased in any way. This sounds more difficult than it is. The key is being open to the fact that any substance could elicit a positive or negative reaction in the body under different circumstances. Sugar may test negative the vast majority of the time in people, but it could be a lifesaver for someone with mismanaged diabetes. Organ meats are wonderful in general, but if the body is ready to cleanse or is severely fat intolerant, organ meats could tax the body unnecessarily.

I do not assume to know. I let the person's body, or my body, speak, and I simply translate. I began vibrationally testing foods on myself, my husband, and my daughter on a daily and meal-by-meal basis. I found that the body's needs can change gradually or quite rapidly. When the body was low in a mineral, vitamin, or specific amino acid, it could take many meals to bring the nutrient back into balance, and other times, it would take only one serving of a food.

About the same time, I discovered Weston A. Price's research, which stated that organ meats and seafood were prevalent in primitive diets. He also emphasized the importance of raw dairy products, so I began to vibrationally test everyone I knew for pasteurized and unpasteurized cow and goat's milk. My vibrational tests largely matched Price's findings, which spoke to the ills of pasteurization. I did not find a single person who tested positively for pasteurized cow's milk. In fact, I found that even raw cow's milk products were vibrationally deadening for over half of the people I tested. Everyone I tested was positive for raw goat's milk.

There is no set or fixed diet for perfect health. The Equilibrium Diet uses a few flexible rules to reawaken the instincts, which will always reveal your individual truth. Once you unlock your instincts and can use your body as a truth detector, you know immediately what foods, herbs, medicines, and vaccinations are, or are not, in your highest and best interest—you awaken the ability to *know* you have a food intolerance before suffering through the painful consequences of eating the food.

So if we all have these instincts and are able to reestablish our connection with them, what happens when you do not listen to your instincts? Well, it depends on the situation, but it will always cost you something! The cost could be a kid with a scraped knee, or a scratchy throat, or feeling like you have a hangover. At the extreme, I have spent entire days in pain, because I did not want to "waste" foods that I shouldn't have eaten, foods that weren't vibrational matches for me.

Hopefully, you can learn from my painful mistakes and not have to suffer your own. This is a very different model for those of us who grew up with the mentality, "No pain, no gain." This is not the case for vibrational nutrition—trust your instincts and vibrational testing; the ego does *not* know better. Vibrational nutrition strips away all complication and confusion—it simply asks the body what it wants. You do not need to know what doctors, or nutritionists, or special interest groups, or I say you should eat—you know in each moment what is good for you, what tips you toward the vibration of health. There is nothing simpler or more profound than our instincts.

Finally, many people ask me, "How long does it take to reawaken the subtle instincts of the body and be able to use them once we begin eating well?" I think the timeline largely depends on how open to the idea of instincts we are. For most people, three months to three years will be enough time to awaken the energetic body and remember how to use their instincts. The more open and embracing of our instincts, the faster and easier we rediscover them. I probably had the ability to use my instincts after three months but did not accept them and open up to them for about two years. Lance probably had the ability after six months but did not accept his instincts until two years on the diet. Understand that if you choose to pursue the path of health, your instincts cannot be blocked forever—continuing to block the instincts will cause extreme emotional distress.

* * *

Everything is a vibrating field of energy—the human body is an energetic body. As energetic bodies, we interact with all of the energy around us—including food. It is not that sugar and processed foods are "good" or "bad" or that God likes some foods and dislikes others—different foods simply have different effects on the body; depending on which effect we want, we choose different foods. If we want to block our true feelings, pain, and desires, we invest in ice cream, candy, and processed food. These foods make the third dimension feel more "real" or "solid" instead of energetic and vibrational. Large amounts of these food groups make us more forgetful of our spiritual nature because of the stress on the body, brain, and emotions. Sugar and processed foods operate at a different frequency than organic liver and cooked carrots in the body. When the former interacts with the body, it makes the body less conductive; that is, energy moves more slowly and does not transmit as quickly. Foods with easily absorbable minerals make the body more conductive; this is important because the body is both an electrical conductor and an electrical system.

Just as metals are good conductors of electricity, so are we when we eat certain foods. This is why mineral content and growing foods in mineral-rich soil is so important. We can think of two human bodies as two different electrical systems that run power through grids. The first system, or body, is high in processed food and sugar and thus suffers from a high level of "line loss," because it's a poor conductor. Line loss occurs when energy or power is leaked out of the system as it is transported from one place to another. The body becomes a poor conductor of energy, because the system loses energy throughout the day and experiences the depletion of digestive enzymes—nutritional bankruptcy sets in. The other system, one with a diet high in easily absorbable minerals, vitamins, and amino acids, transports information much more efficiently and has very little line loss—all digestive "costs" are investments well suited toward supporting, nourishing, and cleaning the system.

In summary, to become physically healthy, we would like our electrical system to be functioning at the highest level possible. This means that we are conducting and moving energy at a high rate (minerals promote this) and that we are essentially a closed-loop system—meaning we have very little line loss so that minerals that enter our system stay in our system and are not leaked out in any way. In both cases, we are full of energy and *remain* full of energy—at this pinnacle, all energy goes toward propelling us toward our heart's desire.

CHAPTER 12

The Second Enlightenment

I had made my peace with the Universe, and I had accepted its mission for me. Like it or not—in sickness and health, for better or worse—I had given up fighting what I was told that I was here to do. I had a good job that paid well, and I had enjoyed it, but the tides were shifting, and it was not enough for me anymore. I had to write. I had this bug inside of me that was scratching to get out, and it seemed that the only way to silence it and get some peace was to show up to the keyboard and type every day. I had embraced change; I had embraced death—I was still filled with fear, but I had begun chipping away at the mountain.

I had not breathed a word of my experiences to anyone but Lance in three years. Three years after my first enlightenment experience, I finally told my parents. I told them what had happened. I told them what I was here to do, and I told them about the book. They didn't laugh or think I was crazy. My mom cried—I cried. They wanted to know more. Slowly, I began telling a few people—I began speaking my truth. To my amazement, no one ridiculed me. No one called me crazy. Everyone was incredibly supportive. Some had spiritual stories of their own to share, and everyone wanted to know more. What did I feel? What did I learn? Was it truly tied to diet? Could they do it too?

Telling a few close friends gave me the courage to do what I knew I needed to do—I knew I needed to tell the people I worked with. I was teaching finance at a local university, and I was afraid to tell my senior faculty members about my experience and the book I was told to write. I knew how I would have reacted to such a story just three years ago, back when I was only living in my left brain. I would have thought the person was crazy. I saw my colleagues as my extended family, and I cared deeply about each of them; for them to "not believe" me, or think differently of me, was a terrifying thought for me. I was afraid they would not accept me for who I really was. My fear of not being loved unconditionally was popping up again, and I had to make the decision to tell them and be my authentic self rather than suffer to maintain some image that I *thought* they had of me. The rest would be up to them. I knew telling them was part of releasing my fear—it was hard, and I felt myself procrastinating. Then I remembered the will and determination I had perfected through years of early morning volleyball practice, long hours as an investment-banking analyst and PhD student. I was tenacious. And for the first time in my life, I was going to use that determination to catapult me toward the Universe's path for me, instead of away from it. Just as I had gotten up at 4:00 a.m. to pick weeds out of Idaho wheat fields, I set a date and time that I would tell my colleagues—I would make myself.

The day came, and I was a nervous wreck. I sat in my car and tried to get my sister to give me a pep talk. I was so afraid they would laugh at me. Or tell me I needed professional help or even fire me. After all, this wasn't standard academic theory I was dealing with here. My journey could be a path that the department and the university simply would not support—I was fully prepared for the worst, but I knew it had to be done. This was the Universe's path for me, and I was trusting that everything would work out for the best, whatever the best may be. For the first time in my life, I felt my own nervous energy around me. It seemed stronger than the nervous energy I felt from other people. It wasn't as scattered; it felt more uniform or wavelike. I realized I was nervous because I really cared—I cared about following my apparent path; I cared about the people I worked with, and I was nervous because I didn't know if the two could coexist.

I told myself that I was courageous and I must use my courage now. I told myself, "Deep down you know you can do it; your ego is getting in the way. It is telling you every reason to be afraid and to succumb to your fear. Just for this week, put your ego in a black box in your mind and see what happens. In doing this, you are not allowing yourself to be afraid of anything.

"You will approach the world in a state of wonder and awe like a small child. You will be curious about everything and fear nothing. You will approach everything knowing it was created in love. This is why you have learned about your strength and power over the years. You are to use that strength now toward your true goals instead of toward your ego, which ultimately will block your highest self. Your will stands between you and your dreams. Your fear blocks you from your goals. This is the season of change and death, the death of your fear. You will release it and find peace."

I embraced my mission. I walked boldly across the parking lot and into the building, telling myself that my job here on earth is to shed light on possibilities. To provide people the chance to expand their models, expand their way of looking at the world, to include both sides of the brain and their instincts. What better place to start than with left-brained business professors?

I met with Michael first. He was a finance geek like me. I confessed that I was nervous. I told him everything. I told him about our dietary changes, enlightenment, what I had been working on, and what I had to do. To my amazement, he embraced me just as my parents and friends had. He was even understanding. It was in that moment that I realized that the book wasn't about me; it wasn't for me—the book was for other people. The book was for Michael and all of my other colleagues, and friends, and people I didn't even know. Michael gave me a lot of strength that day. He helped me rediscover my voice. I also knew, hearing his story and his pain, that he could heal by hearing my experience. It didn't matter that I revealed the darkest moments of my life or that I was afraid of people judging me—through those painful, dark experiences, perhaps others can heal too. We all go through incredibly emotional experiences in this dimension; we put ourselves through painful events. Those who have had the darkest of days will hopefully realize that they have developed skills because of their experiences—skills that others might not have. This background, whatever it may be, is needed for each of us to reach our own highest self in the near future.

This book was the Universe giving people hope. And not just hope but a blueprint, a map, to remembering who they really are. If I have to share my story of suffering to help others suffer less, so be it. I fully accept that responsibility. If this story can help just one person, it is worth the risks I have taken. My perspective changed. The job of writing that once seemed like a burden instantly became a gift, a gift for which I was only the vessel. I began to look upon my journey with gratitude and awe instead of resentment. This generated a powerful shift in my reality.

One by one, I told my colleagues. I took the proverbial leap of faith—I leapt, and my colleagues caught me. To my surprise, they all embraced me.

They supported me, and they applauded me for having the courage to follow my path. I felt so relieved, I felt so free. It was as if the energy in my throat that had been held back after years in the dark was released, and I was finally able to speak my truth. I could feel the blockages—the knots in my throat and larynx area—being pulled apart. Energy strand by energy strand, my throat began to clear that day. It was like a river gradually pushing through a mound of rocks or leaves that have been slowing its path—gently but firmly the river flows on and takes the debris with it.

* * *

The night after I told Michael, it happened again. This experience was even more amazing than my first enlightenment experience almost three years earlier.

> November 2013. I dreamt I was walking up to my childhood home. A giant male lion ran up to me. I was afraid for a split second, and then I approached him too—I was done being afraid. The lion brushed my chest with his mane and welcomed me and walked with me into the house. It was as if the lion had been waiting there for me my whole life, and I had finally opened up enough to let him in.
>
> Then I was sitting in a kitchen with Lance and an older man I didn't know. I was glad Lance was there, because I was a little nervous. The man telepathically told me he was going to show me where I came from—where we all came from. He very gently placed his hand on my shoulder blade, and an explosion occurred—*boom*. I no longer existed in the physical realm of planet Earth. I was the sea of the universe within all of us, where we are all the same and have no boundaries. I was nothing and everything at the same time. I did not feel like I was a small part of this heaven, I felt like I was heaven; there was no separation, no division.
>
> I felt like a supernova star, everywhere and nowhere all at once. The feeling was simply orgasmic but not in the three-dimensional sense—it was much, much more. It was

an energetic source so powerful and peaceful that I thought, *If this is where we come from, why do we ever choose to leave it for Earth?* It was infinitely expansive, like being the ocean or being outer space, but even more limitless. A glittering yellow-gold universe of possibility. I cannot use three-dimensional words to sufficiently describe it because the Source is not three-dimensional. The Source is peace, rest, renewal, and possibility—latent potential energy; infinite in its own existence.

And then I knew telepathically that we forget our Source when we come into the physical dimension and we feel the illusion of the constraints. As I knew this, I felt the tightness and constriction of the spirit in the third dimension, and I wanted out; I wanted to go back to the yellow-gold sea where I simply "was." The earth bodies forget their infiniteness, wholeness, and peacefulness; we all enter the illusion of confinement. I remembered all the suffering of the third dimension, and I did not understand why it was necessary when we can all go back to this peaceful sea. And then I knew. This yellow-gold sea of everything and nothing is constantly expanding, even though it is already infinite. The only way to expand is to have resistance, or the illusion of something to push against. We and the Source cannot grow and evolve in the connected state of Source. In Source, we just are.

For the universe to continue to expand, people and souls must grow and change. This can only occur in the lower realms, and the physical third dimension is one of such realms. The only way change can occur is through these lower-dimensional "shifts." We always have the option to release our fear and perceived constraints and experience wholeness and oneness again. We choose to take on human form to change and to grow; this is the only way the heavenly sea expands. The more and more we change and grow, the faster and faster the universe outside us and within us expands.

I wondered about some of the higher dimensions and whether or not change occurs there. I instantly learned that higher beings can help us on our paths here in the lower realms, but that they do not change as quickly in the upper realms. The Source inspires humanity to not be satisfied with only the third dimension. To do this, we must first accept all of ourselves and all of our fears. Then we will rise beyond the pain and greet our true selves and love ourselves. When we really love ourselves, we heal—children heal, families heal, countries heal, and the world heals. We all come to earth to experience; sometimes that experience includes healing. Healing is growth. Healing is change. Healing is freedom because we expand ourselves; we expand our probability set—our existence.

Still in the dream state, I wondered, "What should I tell people about my experience and the book—and their future experience?" And I then I understood. I am simply shining light down a different path. We all need to relax, to open, to try. To pretend we are children on the playground who are imagining something "is."

This is creation. Creation is one giant thought.

Imagine this is real. What does it mean for you? How could you change your life? Are you ready? This place, the Source, is within all of us. This is where stars are born. This is what we all are. Source is what each of us *is*. This place, this Source, is all that is real. When fear opens or yields, enlightenment and heaven follow.

This place, Source, is all there truly is—it is *absolute* truth. It is a realm where we are all the same. The Source is the sea, and we are all the drops of water constantly flowing back home. Information travels at speeds much faster than our speed of light; information simply is. We are all born out of that energy, out of the yellow and gold infinite sea of space. This place, the Source, is reality—Earth is the illusion. Earth is the illusion of constraints, the illusion of separation, the illusion of boundaries. None of these are real; we simply forget our Source.

I wanted to stay there forever; I did not want to leave my true home. But then, against my conscious will, I began feeling the constraints of my physical body gradually slide back on as I slowly returned to the world of the illusion.

I realized that the change in diet and nutrition will bring people to the cusp of growth, but each individual must then look in the mirror and see himself. We must each consciously decide to release each fear and tension as it surfaces while the physical body detoxes.

* * *

What does a person do when she sees her origin? What does a person say when she has seen the only thing that is truly real—absolute truth? Objective truth—a concept I, and many others, philosophized to not exist. It is there, nonetheless—whether we admit it or not, Source is there; in fact, Source is all there is. So how does one come back to the illusion? How does one come back to the denseness of Earth? I do not know; perhaps the same way that we came into existence on Earth in the first place, but I simply do not know.

We are all angels that have descended from the Source to help the multiverse grow and expand. So many of us have forgotten. How do you look around the world and see all the pain, all the forgotten love, and not just cry uncontrollably? The truth is that we are all the same; we are all love, and we are all the Source. It is not only that we are connected or similar to each other; we are literally one thing—one Source. We think we are separate; we have forgotten our home, forgotten our nature—forgotten that we are one.

There is no bad or good; there is only forgetting and remembering. When we begin to awaken and stop undertaking behaviors that strengthen our forgetfulness, we begin to unwind the patterns of fear, and we begin to remember. This is not a "fate" game. We can *all* remember. We can all choose to remember, but that is left to our will and our will alone. It is as if all of existence, the Source, were a rainbow, and all of creation are the individual light waves of the rainbow. Today, much of the rainbow is "grayed out" because so many of us have forgotten that we are the rainbow. But there are small patches of remembering, of light and color, where people have rediscovered their nature and are shining their light. When the light waves around this light see the color, they remember their nature too, and they slowly, or instantly, begin to shine their own color. If you remember, the more other people remember—because they see you.

* * *

Seeing the Source changed me. It was a very different experience from the energy download of the first enlightenment. I remembered—I knew.

Instead of just having access to information, I *experienced* the knowledge—I *experienced* the truth—I felt it. Instead of something that happened *to* me, it *was* me. I didn't want to leave. I didn't understand why any of us would choose to leave that place beyond paradise. It was home.

It took several days to distill the information from the Source. Then I snapped out of a quasi-dream state, and the world looked entirely different. Instead of seeing different people, I saw everyone as extensions of myself—just different colors of the same rainbow. In mid-December 2013, I had an epiphany. For so long I had been trying to block different energies and send them away. But I was beginning to wonder if there was more to these energies I was feeling than being just simple random "white noise" of the subtle energy world. I felt like I was being bombarded by other people's problems all the time. It wasn't pleasant, and it made me not want to leave my house at times.

Driving one Saturday morning, I had a flash of insight. Everything happens for a reason; there is a lesson, a learning opportunity in *everything*. The universe sends us exactly what we need to learn. The universe has been bombarding me with energies to get me to *learn* them, to accept them and to understand them. I'd been walking around with my head in the sand like an ostrich, afraid and trying to run from the energies and get rid of them. Now I understand that the universe was sending them to me so that I could learn from them. I realized that my thought patterns were inconsistent. I was accepting that the universe was sending me everything I needed in the physical realm to achieve my goals, but I was not applying that same logic to the energetic realms. I had let other people's perspectives of energies influence my own. So rather than block energies and try to run away, why not embrace them and see what I could learn from them? What better way to do this than to simply ask?

After that epiphany, I started asking. Whenever I felt an energy, I asked it what it was. What better way to learn what energies are, and which are which, than by feeling them and experiencing them and getting to know and understand them? Of course, it's the perfect way to learn—it is the simplest lesson plan imaginable! In one day of simply paying attention to what I was actually feeling, I felt pain, loss, jealousy, rationalization, family stress, holiday stress, work stress. I experienced deep suffering. Humanity suffers so much all the time; we hide our suffering from others, but it is always there following us—literally shadowing us. We have forgotten our Source; we have forgotten our infiniteness. We all yearn to return to the Source, but we have forgotten that we can create it here and now; Source is always here. The knowledge we seek is always there, just under the surface of our awareness—it flows, and we can dig in, dig down, and tap into it. We can allow our true nature to wash away the rubble that has protected us for so long.

* * *

Several weeks after embracing everything that I was feeling as neutral information, I had another powerful realization. We are here to choose; we choose to accept that we are solely responsible for our life, or we tell ourselves the lie that someone else controls us.

We are creators; we create everything in our reality. If this were not true, then we are simply the pawns of other people, or the gods, and have no choice. Our fate would be determined by others, and they, or the gods, can do anything to us at any time. This world would be chaotic, inconsistent, and unpredictable with effects being observed with no apparent cause. Looking at the world around me and my own journey to health, I see and observe free will. What does free will really mean? Free will means that nothing—and I mean nothing, not even death—happens without our permission. Granted, this permission may not be conscious; our ego may block it, and our subconscious may be generating situations in our life, but nothing happens without our willing it to happen. We are completely responsible for everything in our micro and macro life. This means that no one can take your power, your choice, your love from you without you willingly giving it to them.

This is a huge reality shift. Anytime we turn on the television, we bombard our subconscious with victim consciousness. Many of us, myself included, get power (or energy) from playing the role of the victim. Unfortunately, this is ingrained in most of us from a very young age. For example, as a child, your big sister smacks you and pushes you to the ground, and Mom and Dad come running to you (the victim) to dote on you and make sure you are okay. All of that attention your parents give you in that situation is energy, and the scenario continues throughout our lives. If we are divine beings, as Source, we choose everything; there are no exceptions. Exceptions cannot exist—because one exception, one slipup, and we wouldn't be divine beings. Source doesn't make mistakes; you are Source, so you don't either!

I realize people are going to ask, "But what about all the bad crap in the world—all the crap I've gone through?" And I agree, our world could be a much nicer place; however, the world is in its current state because most people do not know their subconscious brain. The subconscious is the storage house, or the software running us and shaping our reality. We create our lives with this programming; so if we don't know, or don't like, what's in there, we are going to end up with surprising or unsatisfactory experiences. If we consciously tell ourselves that we are powerful and intelligent, but our subconscious is running the program that we are weak and stupid (perhaps a program from elementary school), then we will feel weak and stupid and create scenarios to feel that way. Why? Because the subconscious is always running, even when we sleep—it includes about 90 percent of the brain compared to the conscious 10 percent part. Even with affirmations in this scenario, the best you can do is hope to add an additional program to your subconscious that says you are powerful and intelligent, and then both programs will compete for energy, or you will feel conflicted about how to feel when situations arise.

In the physical world, the equivalent would be to turn on your computer and rename your computer's Word application Excel. Yes, you have consciously renamed the program, but every time that program gets triggered, every time you open it up, the program is still going to do everything that Word does. Why are we surprised when we consciously try to impact something that is being driven by the subconscious and don't get the results we want? The only way to get different results is to go in and delete Word from the subconscious entirely, add a new program called Excel, and begin using that. This might sound a bit odd, and it is beyond the scope of this book, but it is doable. Reprogramming the subconscious is essentially what I help people do in the EQ Boot Camp courses, and it is the key to living the life we desire.

CHAPTER 13

The Challenge

A year before our dietary changes, Lance and I were playing golf, eating fast food, drinking beer, and shopping for country club memberships in our free time. Today, Lance still plays golf, I meditate daily, and both of us feel the emotions and illnesses of the people and animals around us. We feel which foods, emotions, and thoughts are in our highest interests and which are not. We do not worry about things like getting sick or having an accident, not because it may never happen but because we realize that if anything happens, it is because we have created that experience, and we trust ourselves to learn from it.

As Source, we are creators, and everything we see around us is a product of our thoughts and our creation. There is no inherent good or bad; there is only a scale of our own preferences. Which things, which foods, which feelings do we choose? McDonald's or homemade organ meatloaf? Each choice creates what we become tomorrow.

I think it would be nearly impossible for someone to experience what I did and not have some desire to just go home to the Source and leave this painful illusion. I teeter-tottered back and forth between wanting to go back to Source and feeling a relentless sense of urgency to help others remember their own truth. There were times when my emotions, my thought forms, and my very being were shifting so quickly that I thought the very ground beneath my feet was crumbling. In a way, it was—the old, shoddy foundation of my being was being replaced with something solid, something true, and something infinite—Source.

Finishing this book has been a relief in many ways. I don't know how my wonderful husband put up with me over the past two years. I was constantly brooding. Always thinking about the book and getting it done. I had to finish writing just to get it out of my head. I felt like I was behind in the Source's schedule for me. I wasn't sure how I was going to do it. My left brain still wasn't keen on talking about everything. I was an academic and a very amateur writer, but I was ready to hunker down and begin my mission.

There were many moments of doubt. But one day, I looked back over the months, the years, of searching, and I realized that I had created something that other people did not yet know existed—I had rediscovered the way humans were intended to eat, an Equilibrium Diet that would lead to vibrant health for anyone. This could really help people. Now I had a sliver of peace too. Ultimately, I knew that Source would lead the way because this was my path—my design. I knew I had made choices and created something that made me feel really good and would do the same for other people.

* * *

Empirically, I am one data point. I understand the skepticism that may arise when people are looking at a single data point; this is why I challenge you to collect more data. Why not devote ninety days of your life to *knowing* and follow the cleanses and diet that Lance and I did. Let's see what happens when more people try the Equilibrium Diet; let's collect more data.

Challenge yourself, challenge me—and make the dietary change of a lifetime. Imagine where you could be if you were using all of your energy toward your life goals instead of just whatever small percentage of your power you have left after keeping up with day-to-day baggage.

There is much to digest. You now have an additional observation in the dataset of your life—an outlier. What are you going to do with this observation? Throw it out? Keep it for later—letting it marinate in the back of your brain? Or will you use it to learn even more information about this new world around you and to point out the limits of your current model? The latter is scary. It means being open to having been wrong all these years. As a beloved mentor of mine always said, "It takes a model to beat a model." Will you choose to remain in the shadows now that you have glimpsed something more?

If you feel disbelief or disregard, you are like I was before this journey of awakening began—your left brain says, "This story just isn't possible. It's an interesting tale, but the author is either lying or crazy." I get it—it is a lot to handle. Believe me, I know—imagine if it happened to you! Only the truth has been written, and sometimes the truth is hard to hear. This book is here to shake you awake. You have brought it into your experience because somewhere inside of you, you know you are ready to remember the truth. Besides, I'm an economist. Have you ever met an economist? We are intensely dry and boring by nature. For me, an atheist economist, to create such a creative tall tale about a world I vehemently didn't believe in ... well, for that to have happened, the inspiration would have had to come from another realm.

I share my story because I have to share it. I was told to do so, and I only found peace while I was writing. In those moments, I knew I was on the right path regardless of my fears and the risks. If this story helps one person find herself and find peace, that means less suffering and more truth in the world, and I will be happy.

* * *

Some people may not think they are ready yet, and that is totally fine—it's not my job to convince them. I aim only to shed light on the path; it is up to each of us to look within. I encourage everyone to ask their own questions. People can say that this or that does not "work," but until they try it, they do not provide any data—they just project fear. This is like standing on top of a skyscraper yelling that gravity does not exist but then being too unwilling or afraid to jump off and prove it.

Everyone has the opportunity to learn that this universe is so much more than just a physical reality—we just need to muster the courage to jump. Whether the choice is conscious or subconscious, you either jump or you don't. You, and only you, create your own future. If it is simply not your time, ignore what I say and continue searching. Someday, perhaps this book will magically "pop" back into your life, and then you will know it is time.

For those who are ready, as you read these pages, you realize it could just as easily be your own story—you glimpse your own power—your own potential—and you are ready for what you will find on your own path to remembering. You step forth, not without trepidation but with the courage and wisdom that anything you find was hidden by you, for your own protection at a certain time and space. You are excited, and I am excited for you. Your path may not be easy—change rarely is—but you will live without regrets from now on. We are all moving at our own pace, and we are exactly where we are supposed to be. You have called this story into your life in this particular moment. You have read this book because a part of you yearns to remember—only ninety days stand between you and your truth. You and only you get to choose where you go. I am excited for you because an amazing journey awaits. I look forward to hearing your story. I look forward to you remembering.

* * *

I finished writing *Atheist to Enlightened in 90 Days* in 2014, and in 2015 it was as if my hibernation period, or my period of total aloneness, ended, and I quite suddenly met several other people who had experienced similar experiences of oneness. Additionally, I learned of several existing vibrational medicine techniques—Holographic Health, NAET, and Network Chiropractic, among others. Clearly, I did not discover anything new to planet Earth. My path was simply that I had to learn it all on my own, independently of any teacher or methodology, probably because I was a lifelong cynic, who wouldn't have believed vibrational medicine, or even tried it, had someone else introduced me to it. The great part of this is that there are already many existing support systems for people looking to begin detoxing and the ninety-day program, which will help avoid many of the painful detox symptoms Lance and I experienced. Holographic Health, NAET, and other vibrational practitioners can help you alleviate and avoid most of the uncomfortable detox symptoms. And even without any vibrational support—I would totally do it again. It was so worth it!

PART 2

The Equilibrium Diet

What can you do for ninety days? Nothing? Anything? What if you knew it would take you ninety days to find yourself—would you start looking?

Warning: This will change your life. Known side effects of the Equilibrium Diet include health, energy, weight loss, and enlightenment.

CHAPTER 14

What Is Healthy?

The idea of guaranteed enlightenment is startling. The world has not been ready for a diet of this magnitude until now. You may be experiencing angst in some form—excitement, nervousness, or both. These feelings are healthy and normal. It is fine to feel any way that you do; be gentle with yourself. Part 2 presents the step-by-step information to recreate the ninety-day cleanse that led to health, weight loss, and enlightenment. This is not a diet per se—I am simply reintroducing you to the intuition and natural intelligence of your body and how your body is intended to derive nutrients.

The Equilibrium Diet is for people and families who are ready to take complete responsibility for their own health and reality; it is for people who are sick of being sick, wonder why they are here, and wonder if there is "something more." This is a blueprint to remembering. The Equilibrium Diet is for people who have tried to get pregnant and couldn't, or tried to lose weight but have never been able to keep it off. There are no caloric restrictions in this diet; it is filled with full-fat everything, and one can eat as much as he cares to—equilibrium is abundance. The Equilibrium Diet is a combination of economics, ancestral diets, modern predispositions, and vibrational nutrition. It creates sustainable, vibrant health by providing the maximum amount of absorbable nutrients in a way that is least costly to the body and the liver.

This isn't a quick fix, but it does provide virtually instant relief for many people, because the liver's burden is reduced. It is a long-term lifestyle that works with your body to reach an equilibrium state of health. For me, this meant no more colds, no more sinus infections or allergies, no more chronic fatigue, no more belly fat or gallbladder problems, and no more thyroid problems. When we consume too much toxic material for the liver and body to handle, the body recruits the help of "new employees"—bacteria, yeasts, and viruses, because these little critters *eat* the toxic material. The critters are not the *cause* of any imbalance; they are the *result* of imbalance, and our bodies begin to rely on these critters to dispose of toxic waste. Toxic waste includes refined food products, wheat, sugar, pasteurized dairy, environmental toxins, chemicals (like pesticides, cleaners, and fragrances), and heavy metals. Each of these substances changes the body's molecular structure in some way.

If you choose to embark on this journey, the key is adhering to the new diet and lifestyle for the full ninety days. It takes ninety days to destroy your old, unhealthy patterns and replace them with new healthy patterns. You may change quickly or slowly, but the key is reprogramming yourself for ninety days—then you will be on the path to health, to happiness, and perhaps even enlightenment. The following regimen leads to results. I have summarized our steps to *remembering* while eliminating entire lists of illnesses and health complaints.

* * *

Before we talk about the Equilibrium Diet and cleanses, I want to make a distinction between "healthy" and "unhealthy," because many of us have been taught that some illness is "normal." We can think of what healthy means by knowing what healthy is not. I make this distinction because had someone asked me five years ago if I was healthy, I would have said yes. But I had a very limited view of what health was. The word "healthy" in our culture no longer means "full of life" and "radiant" or the "complete lack of disease." Most people I speak with have visible health problems yet tell themselves they are healthy. This is not positive thinking—it is denial. We would not call a business that has debts far exceeding its assets healthy—we'd call it insolvent; in other words, *bankrupt*.

The truth is, we could all be a *lot* healthier, and now we have the opportunity to embody a new higher state of wellness. You may have some or many of the following conditions and histories listed below; this list is not meant to judge or criticize—it is here to shake you awake. Remember my *long* list in part 1? We all have to start somewhere! Illness is neither bad nor good; it simply presents us with a learning opportunity. A list of illnesses is sort of like a financial statement, particularly the balance sheet, for the body—it shows us a snapshot of where we are and what needs to change to reestablish *nutritional solvency*. Today, we have the chance to change—sometimes it takes realizing how far from health we actually are to decide to do something about it.

You are *not* healthy if you have *any* of the following:

- allergies (to either seasonal pollens, mold, pets, dust, etc.)
- you take or have taken an antibiotic
- prostate/menstruation problems
- skin rashes/eczema/psoriasis/dermatitis
- sinus problems
- swollen lymph nodes
- constipation (bowel movements less frequently than one per day)
- fatigue or a need to sleep more than eight hours a night
- migraines
- diabetes and on insulin
- depression/mental disorders
- overweight/obese
- autoimmune disorders
- thyroid problems
- you take *any* pharmaceutical drugs
- you take *any* over-the-counter drugs (This includes Advil, Tylenol, and the generic equivalents.)
- you have an addiction (smoking, caffeine, tobacco, food, sugar, exercise, sex, work, gossip, negativity, etc.)

Everyone will start the detoxification process at a different stage, and most people will need to repeat everything several times. This is part of the journey, and yours will be unique. Now that we have defined what healthy is and is not, I want to talk about the motivation part—why do you want to be healthy? Or if you don't think you want to be healthy right now, I want to outline just a few of the benefits for you. As people get healthier and healthier, they experience the following in their lives.

1. High energy levels. Truly healthy people have more energy than they need to complete their day in an enjoyable fashion without relying on stimulants to keep going (caffeine, sugar, etc.) and depressants to relax (alcohol, pharmaceuticals, etc.).
2. Crystal-clear thinking and enhanced mental acuity. Healthy people quite literally have more brainpower—what will you do with your extra brainpower?
3. The body and immune system are healthy. Healthy people rarely, if ever, get sick. What is it worth to always be well? To always feel physically good?
4. Less fear. Healthy people experience less fear due to enhanced brain capacity and an understanding of the harmony of all things. They realize the diseases that many people fear are simply physical manifestations of the mental and emotional bodies and so are not afraid of becoming ill. There are two points to this; healthy people are unlikely to contract a terminal illness, and even if they did, they would mentally approach it as a learning opportunity so they are not afraid of "diseases." What is it worth to always be well? To know your *children* are healthy?
5. Feeling and looking beautiful. When you are healthy, you are at your best physically and mentally, and you feel beautiful/handsome.
6. Increased levels of financial wealth. Healthy people are in a constant state of expansion whereas unhealthy people are in a state of contraction. We each fall somewhere along the continuum in this physical realm of total expansion (oneness) to total contraction (physical death). But when your health is balanced, your mind and emotions must be balanced too, and this ties directly to our sense of power and security and wealth in the world. In general, the healthier you get, the wealthier you'll get. This is not to say that all financially wealthy people are healthy—it is very possible to be wealthy and not healthy. Wealth is driven by our subconscious thought forms just like anything else. As we detox, unhealthy subconscious patterns are weeded out and eliminated. There is nothing we "must do"; it happens naturally as we come more into alignment with Source.
7. Mind-blowing sex. Wait, in case you missed this last one—true health and balance coupled with the right partner leads to mind-blowing sex. Does the partner have to be healthy too for this? I don't know.

> I've never tried it with someone unhealthy! For healthy people, as the physical and emotional bodies return to balance, sex becomes a full body, mind, and spirit experience. When you attain this level of health, you remember why you left Source and chose to come to Earth!

Okay, I know that was a lot to handle. If that didn't get your blood pumping and get you all juiced up to get healthy immediately, you may want to check your pulse and make sure it's still there! Okay, we know you have great stuff in store for yourself—now just hold onto that enthusiasm to propel you through the next chapter: "The E word—Enemas"!

CHAPTER 15

The "E" Word—Enemas

Look, I get it, most of us do not consider enemas luxurious or relaxing or even a part of everyday life. Many of us have spent much of our lives trying to avoid enemas, either in the hospital before having a baby or a medical procedure, or from the prying eyes of our grandparents who wanted to make sure we had our daily BM (bowel movement). Others of us don't even know what an enema is, or we have a biased preconception, without ever having done one. In short, enemas are one of the valuable healing remedies we have forgotten with the rise of modern medicine. For those who do not know, an enema is a liquid solution of some kind inserted rectally into the colon. It is different from colonic irrigation; colonics continually flush the water in and out of the colon with the goal of eventually filling the entire large intestine with water to flush toxins and encourage peristalsis. Peristalsis is the contracting spasms a healthy colon has that encourage the elimination of fecal matter. Most enemas target the four to six inches of the large intestine closest to the rectum—most enemas are used to stimulate peristalsis and relieve constipation, but the coffee enema is a bit different.

The coffee enema creates a sort of magnetic attraction with the toxins in the liver and gallbladder and draws those toxins out and into the colon for immediate elimination. This is a form of dialysis or filtering of the blood, because the liver cleanses all of the blood approximately every four minutes. During a twelve- to fifteen-minute coffee enema, the liver is dumping toxins into the colon from the blood for the duration of the enema.

The coffee enema is loved by all who are brave enough to try it. Several stories say that it was discovered somewhat by chance in battlefield hospitals during World War I and was found to reduce pain in patients almost as effectively as intravenous morphine. Supposedly, German research from the 1920s on rats shows that rats given coffee enemas produce 800 percent more glutathione than rats not given coffee enemas, and a 2002 study also using rats supports even more benefits to coffee enemas than just increased glutathione.[1] (I have no idea how one would give a rat a coffee enema, but I would be interested to learn.) Glutathione is one of the best detoxifying agents in the body. Drink a glass of wine or diet soda, smell some gasoline fumes or bleach, and the liver will have to produce a molecule of glutathione for every molecule of the nasty stuff that has entered your system. Glutathione is *powerful*; it neutralizes just about anything. Intravenous glutathione has been used for years in alternative medicine as an effective method to eradicate some cancers.

Now, let's talk about coffee enemas. Coffee enemas encourage your liver to eliminate its current load of toxins *and* to produce more glutathione. This is a miracle cure when you have a hangover, or a detox headache, or the flu, or have just had anesthesia, or taken any synthetic drug. The coffee enema provides virtually instant relief. The relief will last as long as the body's current toxic load remains below the liver's ability to produce glutathione. For people with heavy toxic loads, this means they could benefit from doing four, six, even ten, coffee enemas per day to reduce liver stress.

Coffee enemas have completely eliminated my pain on too many occasions to remember: from allergies, colds, flu, injuries, and muscle soreness. Once you are in pain and finally muster the courage to try one, you will be hooked—coffee enemas are *that* effective. For people looking to detox, get healthy, and lose weight, coffee enemas help with each of these. Worst-case scenario, a coffee enema forces you to lie down for fifteen minutes per day and *relax*. Coffee enemas are an almost daily occurrence in our household, and we enjoy every minute! So let's get to it.

What is the best way to do a coffee enema? Some people prefer the morning, some the evening, some multiple times per day. Regardless, there are a few things to remember in preparation.

1. Bring the water and coffee to a boil together. Use approximately one heaping tablespoon of *organic caffeinated* coffee per cup of *filtered* water. Boil for fifteen minutes and allow to cool to a comfortable temperature. Decaffeinated coffee will not work and is laced with the

chemicals used to decaffeinate it. Tap water is chlorinated and will kill off beneficial intestinal flora.

2. Always use a three- to four-minute cleansing enema (eight-ounces of plain distilled water, lemon water, or sea salt water) before the coffee enema; this will make the coffee easier to retain for the full twelve to fifteen minutes.
3. Warm enemas are generally easier to retain. Use a disposable enema bottle or an enema bag or bulb to insert one to two cups of the strained coffee into the rectum. Lie on your right side and retain for twelve to fifteen minutes; then expel. If you do not feel the need to use the restroom immediately, that is fine; simply continue with your day until the urge comes naturally.

When using only one to two cups, the coffee doesn't reach far enough into the colon to interfere with electrolyte and mineral absorption in any way. The caffeine in the coffee should not be absorbed if the enema remains in the last several inches of the colon. If you do feel the effects of the caffeine, prepare your coffee with less than one heaping tablespoon per cup of water and only perform the enema in the morning. (Please note that people adhering to Gerson therapy for holistic cancer treatment use up to thirty-two ounces of coffee per enema, instead of one to two cups. This can provide extra detoxification, but I find one to two cups is plenty for me.) In extreme detox cases, a green enema implant can be used to complement coffee enemas.

The Quick and Easy Coffee Enema: On many occasions, I have needed a quick and easy coffee enema. In these cases, I skip the cleansing enema and use regular coffee brewed in a coffee pot. I do notice a difference in effectiveness, but it still provides relief—better some coffee than none!

Implants

Enema implants also aid in detoxification. Typically four ounces of a raw green fluid (wheatgrass juice, blue-green algae, kale juice) is mixed with one cup of distilled water and inserted rectally. This implant is left in and absorbed through the colon wall. Ideally, implants are completely absorbed by the colon and *never* expelled. Always do an implant *after* a cleansing enema to make sure it can be retained and absorbed. Implants are great for people with absorption problems because the blood receives the nutrients directly from the colon instead of the small intestine. During times of heavy detox, one to two implants can be inserted daily. Implants are more nourishing than a coffee enema, which strictly eliminates toxins. If you would like to do a coffee enema and a green implant in the same day, simply be sure to do the coffee enema before the green implant to ensure the implant has adequate time to be fully absorbed.

CHAPTER 16

The Equilibrium Diet: A Blueprint for Transformation

When you eat is just as important as what you eat!
Reduce the burden on your liver; don't eat heavy proteins at night!

Sugar, chemicals, preservatives, and GMOs (foods that have been genetically modified) are all new additions to the food supply. Genetic and dietary evolution for humans happens slowly, with very small changes occurring in a 5,000-year span. Our digestive capabilities are no different from, and definitely not better than, our ancestors from 5,000 years ago. The man-made changes and shifts in the food supply have outpaced our body's natural evolutionary process; for this reason, the ancient ways of eating most complement the body's digestive capabilities. When the body does not recognize a substance as food, it will not digest the substance; instead the body will try to neutralize, destroy, and eliminate what it considers to be toxic. When the body does not have the enzymes and antioxidants to neutralize and destroy toxins, it will store the substances away until the given detoxifiers are available. This "storage" can lead to excess weight, obesity, and a host of illnesses as the body invites viruses, bacteria, and yeasts to eat the waste and its by-products. What we call disease is simply a symptom, or a side effect, of having large stores of waste in the body—once the waste and toxic material are removed, the critters simply die or leave.

Our ancestors just a few hundred years ago ate about ten times more fat than we do today, and they were skinnier and healthier! Fat contains essential fat-soluble vitamins that the vast majority of us severely lack. It is estimated that almost all Americans are deficient in vitamin D, and vitamin A is quickly rising to the same status. The fat-soluble vitamins A, E, and D are required for proper functioning of the immune system, reproduction system, brain and central nervous system, and the skin. Deficiencies in any of these fat-soluble vitamins in utero lead to birth defects and death in animals and humans.[1] Vitamin K, the final fat-soluble vitamin, is needed for strong bones and to clot blood.

One of the great things about the Equilibrium Diet is fat! And loads of it! So yes, you are going to eat a lot of fat: butter, coconut oil, avocados, even bacon and animal fat. Eat sourdough toast slathered with raw butter as thick as you can stomach it—feast on cholesterol-rich lobster, crab, shrimp, and organ meats. Enjoy homemade sugar-free Jell-O, fruit snacks, and marshmallows. Use raw whole milk and cream generously—just avoid fried and trans-fats because both are rancid and toxic to the body. Rancidity occurs when the fat or oil is exposed to high temperatures or when it ages and begins to decompose—the molecular structure degenerates, producing a rancid odor and taste. The keys to the Equilibrium Diet are quality inputs and the quality processes: timing, food preparation, and seasonality.

1. Certain foods should be eaten at certain times of the day and avoided at other times.
2. Many foods like nuts, seeds, and grains require special preparation like soaking, sprouting, and fermenting to ensure proper nutrient absorption. All nuts, seeds, rice, beans, corn, and wheat should be soaked overnight and fermented, or sprouted before cooking.
3. Certain foods should be consumed during certain seasons and avoided during other seasons.

To summarize, we should eat what our ancestors ate and how they ate; if our ancestors didn't eat it, we shouldn't either. The goal of the Equilibrium Diet is to provide the body with a balance of nutrients so that it can work as efficiently as possible. Much of this lifestyle change involves recreating how our ancestors ate; however, it differs from the mainstream ancestral diets in the timing of when certain foods are consumed and how foods are prepared.[2] The timing of *when* you eat *what* is just as important as *what* you eat. Optimal food consumption during the timeline of a day works with the body's digestive abilities and pH cycle to minimize the waste created. The impact of the pH cycle was first recognized by Dr. Wheelwright and then recorded in *The Pro-Vita Diet* by Jack Tipps, NE and PhD.

The Equilibrium Diet will catapult you out of nutritional bankruptcy and will awaken your instincts—you will begin to sense what works best for *you*. Listen to your body—you may not be able to hear it now, but after ninety days on the Equilibrium Diet, your body will start talking to you. It will say, "Give me raw salads. Give me sprouted seeds." Or, "The thought of raw foods or red meat makes me nauseous." You are the ultimate source of truth; the Equilibrium Diet just helps you remember. The following chart lists the nine overarching principles of the Equilibrium Diet. These are the nine high-quality processes that clean up our nutritional financial statements (those illness and symptom lists we all have) and push us toward not just nutritional solvency but extreme *profitability*.

The Nine Principles of the Equilibrium Diet

1.	The body needs to be in an acidic state to properly digest proteins, so proteins should be eaten before 2:00 p.m.
2.	Fruits and natural sugars should not be consumed before 2:00 p.m.
3.	Avoid eating proteins and carbohydrates together to increase the amount of protein your body is able to use.
4.	Avoid eating anything besides fruit after 7:00 p.m.
5.	Eat as much organic fat as you possibly can.
6.	Consume as many of the super-foods as you possibly can: organ meats, unpasteurized milk, all foods from the ocean, and fresh raw juices.
7.	Consume fermented and cultured foods daily.
8.	No caffeine, alcohol, or sugar of any kind—except fruit. No refined products: white flour, pasta, processed foods, or anything that comes premade.
9.	Drink pure filtered water.

Let's discuss each principle.

#1. The body needs to be in an acidic state to properly digest proteins. The pH cycle of the body is set by nature but can be weakened by a diet with poor timing. This means that proteins should be eaten in the morning when the body's pH cycle is at its most acidic peak. Protein should not be consumed after 2:00 p.m. when the body cycles into its alkaline phase. The liver knows which "projects" it wants to undertake, and in which order, but when it is only given a few amino acids, it may have to go manufacture some other amino acids just to use what it has been given. Different proteins, like beef, milk, eggs, and nuts, each have different amino acid profiles. To prevent the liver from "gathering and stripping" amino acids from the rest of the body, we have to provide it with the entire spectrum of amino acids in each protein-dense meal. This is accomplished by eating three to five *different* sources of protein *together* during breakfast and lunch. This minimizes the workload of the liver. With three to five sources of protein, the liver is given a complete profile of amino acids and can rearrange them into whatever structure it needs.[3]

Avoiding proteins past 2:00 p.m. is *one of the most important* aspects of the Equilibrium Diet. This frees the liver to clean at night while you sleep. The toxic load of the body is reduced, and you feel better with cumulative results. The longer you eat like this, the better you will feel. When you are "not hungry" in the morning, you have eaten too much the night before. This is a sign the liver is congested and still struggling with the last meal. Listen to your body. If you are not hungry in the morning, cut back on your evening consumption. One of the easiest ways to set the pattern of eating proteins for breakfast is to skip dinner. Fast after 2:00 p.m. or simply have a small dinner of fruit—do this for as long as needed to regain the urge to eat upon waking.

#2. Fruits and natural sugars should not be consumed before 2:00 p.m. These foods require an alkaline pH for proper digestion and to minimize stress on the body. This completely stabilizes the body's blood sugar and is wonderful for hypoglycemia and diabetes. This diet keeps blood sugar moderate, stable, and steady all day long. You can feel the difference within days of making the switch. Sugar cravings plummet, mood and appetite stabilize, and you feel full until your next meal.[4]

#3. Avoid eating proteins and carbohydrates together to increase the amount of protein your body is able to use. Most people are protein deficient because the body does not absorb proteins well after 2:00 p.m. Most of us consume a lot of protein, but we eat it at dinner. We do not get much out of it because of improper timing. If you are trying to increase your protein absorption, complex carbohydrates like grains and potatoes should be avoided in protein-dense meals.

The body chooses whether to digest each meal as "carb" dominant or "protein" dominant, and "carb" is the default mode to prevent protein toxicity. Even slightly too much protein is detrimental to the body, and the carb "default" serves as a stop-guard against protein toxicity. When the body chooses to digest a meal as carbs, the vast majority of protein is not properly broken down and becomes waste in the body that must be eliminated.

#4. Avoid eating anything besides fruit past 7:00 p.m. This allows digestion to be completely finished before we go to sleep. The liver's cleansing and building phase is between 11:00 p.m. and 5:00 a.m. This is when the liver is most efficient at cleaning and repairing the body. If the liver is preoccupied trying to digest a large meal, it gets to spend less time cleaning. This results in liver congestion, lower immunity, and fatigue. The liver's cleansing cycle is almost entirely eliminated when a protein-heavy meal is consumed late at night. If we eat a steak at 9:00 p.m., the liver needs about eight hours to *attempt* to digest it—the liver finally finishes digesting the steak at 5:00 a.m. and does not have a chance to clean.

#5. Eat as much organic fat as you possibly can. Modern science acknowledges that our ancestors ate on average ten times more fat than we do today. This means they received ten times more fat-soluble vitamins (A, E, D, K) than we eat today. When looking at primitive tribes with virtually perfect health, Dr. Price, DDS, found that primitive societies had a *minimum* of 30 percent of their calories coming from fats and up to 90 percent, or more, in cold climates with no ill effects.[5] The fat-soluble vitamins are great immune boosters and blood builders. I recommend organic fats because for animal sources, a lot of toxins are fat-soluble and will be stored in the fat tissues. Ideally, we want minimal exposure to those fat-soluble toxins (most chemicals, plastics, antibiotics, etc.). So go forth and enjoy! Eat chicken skin, gravy (without white flour), grizzle, and butter; load up on your fat of choice! Raw butter and cream are excellent sources of fat-soluble vitamins.

#6. Consume as many of the Equilibrium Diet super-foods as you possibly can: organ meats, unpasteurized milk, all foods from the sea, and fresh raw juices. The four best foods for everyone to eat are organ meats, *unpasteurized* dairy, anything from the sea, and raw juices. Seafood includes sea creatures, sea vegetables, seaweeds, and algae. These foods yield the highest return on investment given the body's cost to digest them. They provide the biggest nutritional bang for their digestive buck. Each food is relatively easy to digest, particularly compared to its substitutes: muscle meats, pasteurized dairy, animal proteins, and vegetables, respectively.

Each super-food provides vast stores of easily absorbable vitamins and minerals. With each food, the digestive work is minimized. This means low digestive cost and high nutrient density. (Note: Many people will not be able to properly digest the casein protein in cow's milk even when unpasteurized. These individuals should rely on raw milk from goat or sheep to minimize the intolerance. See chapter 17, "Controversial Foods," for more information.) These are the major foods that help build and strengthen the body. Without these foods, vitality and health cannot occur. You can cleanse and remove current toxins, and you will feel better, but you will never be able to rebuild the body's lost stores of nutrients on a solely plant-based or raw diet.

This is because the digestive cost of plant proteins and nutrients greatly exceeds the cost of organ meats, raw dairy, and seafood. These food categories are the most nutrient dense *and* easily absorbable foods on the planet. Weston A. Price, DDS, studied primitive people and diets and came to the same conclusion: the healthiest people in the world eat an abundance of at least two of the categories. Blue-green algae like spirulina, chlorella, and E3Live are some of the best detoxifiers and can rid the body of heavy metals and radiation poisoning. Augmenting our diets with fresh raw vegetable juices provides easily absorbable minerals and extra enzymes. This becomes more important the healthier we become and when our bodies seek to build. Because our soil lacks the nutritional value it had even eighty years ago, it can be necessary to supplement our mineral sources, and juicing is an easy way to do this.

#7. Consume fermented and cultured foods daily. All primitive peoples consumed fermented foods like sauerkraut, pickles, kimchi, raw yogurt, kefir, and kombucha on a daily basis. Such foods provide prebiotics and probiotics for healthy intestinal flora. It is important that these products are free of all sugar, dyes, and artificial preservatives—organic grocers offer several good brands. Probiotic supplements are not created equally; a decent probiotic usually needs to be refrigerated. Several good ones that do *not* require refrigeration are ThreeLac and FiveLac by Global Health Trax, which can be ordered on Amazon.com, and Restore™ by Biomic Sciences, LLC.

#8. No caffeine, alcohol, sugar of any kind except fruits. No refined products: white flour, pasta, processed food, or anything that comes premade. Each of these substances depletes the body, because it costs more to digest or neutralize than it provides in nutritional value; anything processed or refined offers virtually nothing in terms of absorbable nutrients. (See chapter 17, "Controversial Foods," for more information.) Each of these pseudo-foods is stressful to the liver and yields a net loss to our overall health *every* time we eat it. Our goal is to minimize our liver's stress load as much as possible. (I recommend avoiding all refined products for ninety days and then adding back a few—like white rice—only if you do not want to properly prepare brown rice to remove the phytic acid.)

#9. Drink pure filtered water. Tap water is particularly bad for the thyroid, which cannot distinguish between iodine, chlorine, and fluoride and will absorb whichever element is present. Drink the purest water you can obtain and afford. We did not switch to filtered water until several months after beginning the diet. I noticed my throat was getting scratchy from the chlorine in the tap water and we began buying filtered water. Listen to how much water your body actually wants; for instance, if you drink three glasses of raw goat's milk a day, you will probably need fewer than eight glasses of water. I recommend drinking a glass of water when you wake up in the morning to prepare your hydration levels for a big breakfast. In general, avoid drinking large amounts of fluids with meals to avoid diluting your stomach acid.

Note: The Equilibrium Diet should be tailored to each individual. This includes the flexibility to eat the percentage of raw and cooked vegetables that feels best for you. There are pros and cons of consuming both raw and cooked vegetables, which will be discussed in chapter 18, "The Low-Down on Other Diets." Ultimately, sometimes raw is preferred, sometimes cooked vegetables are preferred; our bodies always know exactly what they need.

* * *

Meal Ideas

Our goal is to eat what, how, and when our ancestors ate. Getting started and making the switch to eating proteins for breakfast is the hardest part. Once the switch is made, it becomes natural, and we find heavy proteins undesirable at night. Here are some examples of foods for each meal.

For Breakfast and Lunch, Eat Protein and Vegetables.

We are "protein-avoires" before 2:00 p.m.

Nuts and Seeds. Soaked or sprouted and roasted—do not eat raw nuts without soaking them. All raw nuts and seeds have a toxic outer layer, phytic acid, that binds to minerals like calcium and zinc in the human body. Nuts also provide essential fatty acids, which are needed with every meal.
Animal Proteins. Lightly cooked or raw organic eggs, cooked fish, and other animal proteins. Sprouts are also a protein and are packed with enzymes. Common sprouts include alfalfa, sunflower, mung bean, and radish.
Organ Meats and Bone Broths. Organic meats were the prize cuts of our ancestors and were saved for those who needed extra nutrients: parents-to-be, breastfeeding mothers, children, and the ill. These are building foods and were given to tribe members most in need of nourishment. Those of us on the standard American diet are nutritionally deprived and would fall into the category of "needing nourishment."
Cheese. Raw or fresh cheeses like ricotta, cottage cheese, mozzarella, feta, goat, and sheep's cheese. Avoid dairy and wheat products during allergy season, because both dairy and wheat are inflammatory. Goat milk products can typically still be consumed in moderation during allergy season.
Veggies. Choose four to five for each meal to buffer your proteins. Stay away from the heavy starches to keep protein absorption to a maximum. If you are eating a protein-rich meal, avoid corn, potatoes, eggplant, sweet potato, yam, and other high-starch veggies. Do you have to eat four to five vegetables with every meal? No, but it is a good goal. I have eaten just broccoli for breakfast many times!

The goal is to have several sources of protein buffered with cooked or fresh vegetables. The vegetables ensure that an adequate supply of enzymes is available to help break down the protein. Eating just protein without vegetables once in a while is fine, but it is taxing to the system and can result in what Chinese Medicine refers to as "dampness" in the body, particularly in the spleen. Here are some protein-heavy meal ideas.

Breakfast and Lunch Meal Ideas

- steak and veggies with soaked nuts and seeds
- baked chicken *with* skin and veggies, cheese, and almond butter toast
- hamburgers with cheese, sprouts (count as a protein), tomatoes, lettuce, onion, and pickles
- marinated tempeh stir-fried with veggies, feta cheese, and sprouts
- lamb, beef, turkey, or chicken in the slow cooker with veggies (carrots, celery, and onions); side of soaked seeds with herbs, or toast with almond butter or cheese
- omelet with cheese, turkey bacon or shrimp, sprouts and vegetables
- salad with soaked nuts and seeds, cheese, sprouts, and pulled chicken/grilled steak/shrimp/salmon
- breakfast frittata

Dinner (and lunch if you are not trying to build protein reserves) will consist mainly of carbohydrates. Raw dairy products can complement the meal and should be relied upon to minimize phytic acid exposure when grains are eaten, but proteins, especially heavy proteins like meats, should be avoided. When eating out, I follow the "three-bite rule"—I never eat more than three small bites of a protein-rich dish like steak, chicken, or eggs. Fruit should always be consumed by itself and given at least twenty minutes to digest before eating anything else. This will minimize intestinal gas and bloating and ensure you derive nutrients from the fruit.

For Dinner, Eat Fruits and Carbohydrates

We are vegetarians after 2:00 p.m.!

Vegetables—broccoli, kale, cabbage, cauliflower, pumpkin, zucchini, green peas, carrots, potatoes. If it's a vegetable, eat it.
Bread (preferably sourdough) made from spelt, teff, oat, millet, sorghum, and buckwheat.

Brown rice, lentils, quinoa, amaranth, millet. Note: Everything should be soaked for at least twenty-four hours in a warm, acidic, medium-like water with lemon juice, whey, apple cider vinegar, or kombucha before being cooked. Even better is to ferment or sourdough the grains.
Breakfast for dinner: pancakes, waffles, French toast made with sprouted wheat or gluten-free bread. Oatmeal, steel cut oats, buckwheat, or kasha. Buckwheat is actually related to rhubarb and is *not* a wheat. Please note that if you are battling candida, diabetes, or other chronic or acute illnesses, you will want to minimize sugar (even maple syrup), but blackstrap molasses can be a decent substitute for a sweet drizzle. Plain butter is also a great alternative, or you can sprinkle on a little stevia.
Spelt or brown rice pasta—spaghetti, lasagna, rigatoni. Soak these during the day to reduce cooking time and ease digestion. To reduce phytic acid, soak in a warm, acidic medium with some buckwheat or rye flour (1/2 tablespoon per cup) for twenty-four hours.
Salads
Baked potato or sweet potato with trimmings
Rice and veggie stir-fries
Lentil or bean tacos with corn tortillas and goat cheese (Goat cheese ensures the phytic acid is partially mitigated.)

Remember, foods (even bacon) should not contain any colorings, additives, chemicals, or man-made preservatives. For instance, you would not want to eat Yellow 5, monosodium glutamate (MSG), nitrates, or sulfites, but ascorbic acid (vitamin C) or even citric acid would be "okay" preservatives. If you do not know what an ingredient is, do not eat it.

* * *

Afternoon and Evening Snacks

Fresh seasonal fruit is a great snack and should be eaten by itself. Fresh fruit and raw milks require virtually no digestion. Each should be eaten by itself, allowing it to pass quickly into the small intestine for absorption. (For example, you could drink a glass of raw goat milk twenty-minutes before a meal or you could eat a bowl of fresh fruit before dinner, but do not eat fresh fruit and drink raw milk together.) You can eat a few pieces of mango or pineapple after a meal for the enzyme, bentaine, to aid the body in digestion, but all other fruits should be eaten alone. For people requiring extra calories (pregnant or breastfeeding mothers, children), an afternoon snack can also consist of carbohydrates instead of fruit—just no heavy proteins.

The Equilibrium Diet is not based on dieting or portion control. You can eat absolutely as much as you want. If you are hungry, eat; if you aren't hungry, don't eat. Just remember to follow the simple rules:

1. Don't eat proteins and carbs together.
2. Don't eat protein-laden meals after 2:00 p.m.
3. Eat fruits by themselves and not in the morning. (You will be hungry in an hour if you do.)
4. Don't eat dinner after 7:00 p.m. or after four hours before bed. Your liver goes into cleansing mode about 11:00 p.m., so you don't want it preoccupied with digestion when it is supposed to be cleaning house for the next day.

Many people ask, "Isn't it weird to have your big meal in the morning?" Even though almost everyone has heard the old adage, "Eat like a king for breakfast, a prince for lunch, and a pauper for dinner to stay healthy," many people fight the idea; they say they aren't hungry in the morning. When you eat protein at night, that energy is just becoming available when you wake up, and your liver really doesn't want to start digesting all over again. Once you make the switch, you will never want to eat a heavy protein meal at night again; your body will be so in tune with cleansing at night that if you do eat protein, you will feel all the symptoms of a stressed liver the next day or in the middle of the night: back pain, stabbing intestinal pain, bad taste in mouth, headaches, sleepiness and lethargy, joint and muscle stiffness, and more.

On the following pages, I have included three sample days for eating according to the Equilibrium Diet principles. At the end of each protein-heavy meal, I have tallied the number of *different* protein sources and the number of *different* vegetables. Remember, it is important to have several different protein sources to provide the liver with the entire spectrum of amino acids—this minimizes the costs of digestion, because the liver is able to use what it is given instead of having to scour the body to find what's missing in an incomplete amino acid profile. For Equilibrium Diet recipes go to www.equilibriumdiet.com.

SAMPLE DAY 1

7:00 A.M.	1 glass filtered water, 1 glass raw goat milk with blackstrap molasses to taste.
7:30 A.M. BREAKFAST	Frittata with eggs, goat cheese, tomatoes, mushrooms, and turkey bacon topped with sprouts and a slice of gluten-free bread with almond butter. **Count: 6 different proteins, 3 different vegetables (sprouts count as both).**
BEFORE LUNCH	1 glass raw goat milk with blackstrap molasses to taste.
12:30 P.M. LUNCH	Baked chicken with collard greens and okra, baby carrots dipped in cashew butter, and slices of goat cheese. **Count: 3 proteins, 3 vegetables.**
BEFORE DINNER	1 glass raw goat milk with blackstrap molasses to taste.
6:30 P.M. DINNER	Vegetable stir-fry with rice. (Or fresh fruit if you are full). **Count: 0 proteins.**

SAMPLE DAY 2

7:00 A.M.	1 glass filtered water, 1 glass raw goat milk with blackstrap molasses to taste.
7:30 A.M. BREAKFAST	Organ meatloaf topped with turkey bacon and goat cheese, and made with onions, peppers, mushrooms, and almond flour. Side salad topped with sprouts and soaked sunflower seeds. **Count: 6 different proteins, 5+ different vegetables (sprouts count as both).**

BEFORE LUNCH	1 glass raw goat milk with blackstrap molasses to taste.
12:30 P.M. LUNCH	Chicken drumsticks with skins. Caribbean rice and beans with onions, peppers and coconut milk. Side of broccoli with goat cheese. **Count: 3 proteins, 3 vegetables.**
BEFORE DINNER	1 glass raw goat milk with blackstrap molasses to taste.
6:30 P.M. DINNER	Bone broth wild rice with local greens, tomatoes and goat cheese. (Or fresh fruit if you are full). **Count: 1 protein.**

SAMPLE DAY 3

7:00 A.M.	1 glass filtered water, 1 glass raw goat milk with blackstrap molasses to taste.
7:30 A.M. BREAKFAST	Shrimp salad with zucchini, tomatoes, romaine, carrots, sprouts and goat cheese. Soaked sunflower seeds, pumpkin seeds and brazil nuts. **Count: 6 different proteins, 5 different vegetables (sprouts count as both).**
BEFORE LUNCH	1 glass raw goat milk with blackstrap molasses to taste.
12:30 P.M. LUNCH	Turkey and goat cheese sandwich with pickles and tomatoes. Celery sticks dipped in cashew butter. Soaked nuts and seeds tossed with sea salt and chili powder. **Count: 5 proteins, 3 vegetables.**
BEFORE DINNER	1 glass raw goat milk with blackstrap molasses to taste.
6:30 P.M. DINNER	Soaked oatmeal/steel cut oats with raisins, cinnamon, and apple sauce (Or fresh fruit if you are full). **Count: 0 proteins.**

The sample menus are focused on building—hence the high protein content. As we become healthier and healthier, our bodies become more efficient, and our protein needs decline. You can supplement each morning with herbs and algae tailored for you, but strive to get all of your nutrients from foods in whole forms. In general, my family eats a lot of soups and warm grain cereals for dinner in the wintertime and fresh fruits in the summertime. Summer dinners will usually consist only of watermelon, strawberries, and grapes or whatever fruits are locally in season. Dinner should always be the lightest and least digestively taxing meal of the day. If you find yourself voraciously hungry at dinner, try increasing the amount of protein you are eating for breakfast first, and then increase the amount of protein you are eating for lunch too. Also know that it is perfectly fine to have some easy-to-digest proteins for dinner. Proteins like raw cheeses, milks, and yogurts intrinsically have all of the enzymes needed to digest them, so the body isn't exerted. Raw dairy is also digested relatively quickly, which is important at dinnertime because we want digestion completely done by 11:00 p.m. so the liver can spend the night cleaning and restoring the body.

CHAPTER 17

Controversial Foods

Once you can look at or think about a food and *know* how your body responds to it, the need for research and expert opinions is greatly reduced. The Equilibrium Diet will awaken your instincts—then you won't need my experience or anyone's experience but your own. This chapter addresses food categories that tend to be controversial either in modern or alternative medicine. All of the opinions presented here are based on years of research, combined with vibrational testing. When vibrationally testing, I allow my instincts to relay information to me about how different substances interact with a person's body. This is a type of human lie detection; in short, the body unconsciously responds to a series of questions about foods or substances. All information gathered is independent of what the person tested consciously thinks or believes; it's not based on his or her personal likes and dislikes.

* * *

Dairy—*Raw milk is the only milk worth drinking.* In general, goat's milk is easier for humans to digest than cow's milk. This is particularly true for weak or primitive digestive systems, like those found in infants and most people eating sugar and refined foods. Most people understand lactose intolerance, but the peril of dairy is its protein structure. Bovine casein is the protein that constitutes 75–80 percent of the protein found in cow's milk, and it is difficult to digest even in its natural raw state, which includes enzymes and probiotics. Baby cows have four stomachs to digest the raw milk and then, when they are older—alfalfa. When cow's milk is pasteurized, the bovine casein warps, making it virtually impossible for humans to digest; additionally, all enzymes, prebiotics, and probiotics are completely destroyed. When we cannot digest casein, the proteins accumulate as waste in our system, causing inflammation and illness.

In infants, this manifests as colic, ear infections, and/or blood in the stool. This is also the case when the baby is exclusively breastfed, but the mother eats pasteurized dairy. The undigested casein passes through the breast milk to the infant. Babies fed a proper diet will not have any of these symptoms. Remember that wheat and refined products and processed foods can cause stomach upsets in infants as well as adults. All three categories are avoided in the Equilibrium Diet. For anyone with weak digestion, cow's milk products are too difficult to digest properly—this includes raw dairy. Holistic doctors estimate that about 90 percent of Americans have candida overgrowth,[1] which implies weak digestion and low stomach acid levels. I am a huge advocate for raw products and raw milk, but for most of us, even raw diary will end up as waste in the system.

Despite the relative difficulty in digesting casein, raw dairy products are a major source of nutrients for many primitive cultures, as discovered by Weston A. Price, DDS, in his worldwide research in *Nutrition and Physical Degeneration*. Modern society's intolerance to dairy is new. The problem lies partially in the quality of modern dairy products and partially in our lack of digestive robustness; this stems from generations of what Dr. Price calls "the white man's diet"—sugar and refined flour, corn, and rice products. I have vibrationally tested over one hundred people; none tested positive for pasteurized cow's milk. This means that for 100 percent of the men, women, children, and infants I have tested, none of them can properly digest and utilize the cow's milk and dairy products purchased in most grocery stores. Dairy products actually lower and deaden the body's vibration—butter is the only exception, because all of the proteins are removed from the cream in making butter. Most individuals can handle even pasteurized butter, but raw is always preferred.

About 20 percent of people benefit vibrationally from raw cow's milk, and almost everyone benefits vibrationally from raw goat's milk.[2] Compared to our ancestors, the percentage of people able to thrive on raw cow's milk seems to have dropped dramatically. I have several hypotheses as to why dairy is so inflammatory in modern times:

1. Weak digestion. As mentioned above, foods devoid of nutrients like modern wheat, white flour, white rice, sugar of any kind, and processed food tax the digestive system and body. Why? The body spends roughly 80 percent of its energy on digestion. If you are not replacing those nutrients and enzymes used in the digestive process, you deplete your vitality bit by bit with each meal. The body becomes more and more depleted—nutritional bankruptcy sets in, and the body calls in the reinforcements: parasites, viruses, bacteria, and candida (fungus) to break down all of the waste lying around.

2. Pasteurization. All milk was intended to be consumed right from the teat. At the moment of expression, the nutrient content of milk is at its peak. Milk is alive and teaming with enzymes, antibodies, vitamins, minerals, proteins, and sugars. The enzymes digest the protein and sugar in the baby's stomach so that the infant's fragile digestive system will not have to do much work. The antibodies are created by the mother's immune system to destroy anything that she and her baby are exposed to.

When milk is pasteurized, it is heated to high temperatures, sometimes slowly, and sometimes quickly in the case of "flash pasteurization." Theoretically, pasteurization kills off bacteria; unfortunately, it also kills off all of the antibodies, enzymes, and probiotics (the friendly bacteria) and denatures many of the vitamins. For the most part, the minerals, proteins, and sugars (lactose) are left unchanged, while the lactase (which breaks down lactose) has been destroyed. This means that when we drink pasteurized milk, our body must produce all of the enzymes needed to break down lactose and the dairy proteins: whey and casein. On a daily, or even weekly basis, manufacturing enzymes is incredibly taxing on the human system; ideally, most of our enzymes come from our diet. The antibodies that were destroyed with pasteurization can no longer benefit your (or the baby's) immune system for protection against pathogens. This is the reason why every parent knows not to microwave or boil breast milk—we do not want to kill off the good stuff. Unpasteurized or raw products contain all of the enzymes and antibodies that nature intended to help digest milk, so long as the cow is healthy.[3] Raw milk is a super-food! Additionally, modern manufacturing sanitation standards are excellent regardless of whether the milk is raw or pasteurized.

While pasteurized milk "goes bad" and must be thrown out, raw milk sours naturally. Those enzymes start to eat and break down the sugar (lactose), and the raw milk slowly turns from sweet to sour. It is still consumable and makes for great biscuits, pancakes, cheeses, and so on. Pasteurized milk is not a life-giving food and is toxic to everyone I have tested. Ultimately, the question of whether or not to consume raw milk hinges on the answer to the following questions: Do you trust your supplier? And are these organic, antibiotic-free, preferably grass-fed mama cows? If you answered yes, raw milk is for you; if you answered no, you will be healthier avoiding dairy altogether rather than eating *any* pasteurized dairy. Cow, goat, and buffalo milk have been staples of many human diets for thousands of years. Our ancestors did not have the digestive problems modern Americans face with dairy. One of the reasons for this is pasteurization; another is the prevalence of vaccinations.

3. Vaccinations. When a vaccination is injected into the body, it bypasses the body's first line of defense: the eyes, ears, nose, throat, and skin. The first line of defense is what triggers the body to start revving up the immune system. In the first line of defense, the body is feeling out the situation: How strong is this virus? How many viruses are around? How many resources do we really need to spend to avoid this battle? When the vaccination bypasses stage 1, the body gets a signal from its second line of defense. This is out of order for the body, so the immune system thinks the whole house is burning down and tries to attack, attack, attack.

A vaccine pushes the body into a state of panic, a state the body rarely reaches when encountering anything else from the environment. Now, going forward, any time the body encounters the substance in the vaccine, it will react with a similar state of panic. (Note: when something is injected into the body, everything in the injection is treated as a foreign substance; anything in that injection will incite the body to that state of panic—this includes any fillers in the vaccine, any traces of what the vaccine was grown in, and any preservatives used to make sure the vaccine is "sterile." Wheat, egg, and dairy allergies have all skyrocketed in the last half century. Most vaccines are grown in a base of egg, wheat, or dairy. Furthermore, the antibiotics and chemicals used to maintain the vaccine's sterile environment include penicillin and formaldehyde. Formaldehyde is used to preserve dead people; it is a known carcinogen.)

4. Humans have one stomach; cows have four. Cows digest one of the toughest foods on the planet—alfalfa—and to do this, cows have four stomachs. Because of these digestive differences, cow's milk is more difficult to digest than human milk for infants and adults alike. Many other milk types include casein protein, but the bovine variety is the most difficult to digest.

Goat's milk products are actually more common worldwide than cow's milk, and the nutritional profile of goat's milk is more similar to human milk than cow's milk. Furthermore, goats have only one stomach. Raw cow, goat, buffalo, and camel's milk were used by our ancestors worldwide as a staple of nutrition. I hypothesize that weak digestion, pasteurization, and vaccinations all lead to a dairy intolerance. In trying to recreate what our ancestors ate, it may be the case that we are best able to digest what our actual individual ancestors ate as opposed to human ancestors in general. For example, if my descendants came from the Middle East, I may be able to digest raw camel milk perfectly but struggle with raw cow's milk. Those best suited for digesting raw cow's milk may be those individuals whose ancestors thrived on the same thing.

After learning all of this information, many people are probably wondering about themselves and their children—particularly their babies. People wonder if infants should drink raw milk. Well, breast milk is raw! Thank goodness no one has attempted to pasteurize it (well, perhaps formula companies tried)! Mother's breast milk is always best, but if a substitute must be found, raw goat's milk is the best alternative. Raw goat's milk is far superior to pasteurized goat's milk and is easier to digest than raw cow's milk. Infant formulas and pasteurized cow's milk are not nourishing foods—at best, they are stomach fillers, but usually they are toxic, causing ear infections, acid reflux, and a weak immune system. Every baby I have tested would be weakened in some way from eating pasteurized cow's milk or infant formulas. Raw milk for infants and toddlers should be mixed with brewer's yeast, blackstrap molasses, and various essential fatty acids in the form of fresh oils. See www.drmercola.com for the best substitute for human breast milk.

As a side note, allergies and food intolerances are *never* "outgrown." Food intolerances disappear for one of two reasons.

1. The vitamins and minerals needed to properly digest the food have been restored to optimum levels. For instance, magnesium and vitamin F are needed to digest heirloom wheat. Potassium is needed to digest raw dairy.[4] And any emotional triggers have been resolved—this situation will never occur eating a standard American diet.

2. The liver becomes so overburdened that it stops responding to the allergen. This is usually the case with casein and wheat allergies. The liver is so busy trying to survive and deal with the scores of toxins that responding to a food allergy becomes a low priority. Once the liver and body detox and are

able to eliminate some wastes, a fervent reaction will return. The liver is finally able to communicate again, saying, "This food is toxic to me—do not eat it."

* * *

Wheat. The gluten-free craze has made wheat a controversial food. When not properly fermented, wheat is like any other grain or seed and will cause absorption problems in the intestines. Like all refined products, white wheat flour has virtually zero nutrient content. Unfortunately, all wheat has been hybridized in the United States, so it is not what our *grandparents* ate, let alone our ancient ancestors. Spelt is an ancient variety of low-gluten wheat with nine grams of protein per serving as opposed to bread and pasta wheat's two grams. Spelt is much denser, much more nutritious, and, when fermented in sourdough, can sometimes be tolerated even by people requiring gluten-free diets.

* * *

Sushi. Raw meat and fish make up at least some portion of the diet in most healthy primitive societies.[5] Today's nutrition experts vary in their opinions of sushi; some rave about it, while others fear it for potential mercury and parasite content. In general, the more food we can consume from the sea, the healthier we will be. Everything that comes from the sea is soaked and grown in the mineral-rich water known as the ocean. Before modern man's pollution, the sea was a perfect source of nutrient-dense food, offering perfect health. Today, we face a tradeoff between some levels of mercury and parasites and the health benefits these sea creatures offer. I try to eat as much from the sea as possible but also cleanse for heavy metals at least once a year. Parasites are more of an issue in raw fish like sushi. Farmed fish are typically worse for us than wild fish, because farmed fish are not fed the diet found in the ocean. Many farm fish are fed GMO crops (see next section) and laced with colorings to change the color of the meat (in the case of pink salmon). This is a case where our instincts serve us well. If it appeals to you, eat it; if it's not appealing or is off-putting, avoid it. For those who do not yet trust their instincts, or are hesitant, perhaps a wise choice would be moderate sushi consumption coupled with a few parasite cleanses each year.

* * *

Genetically Modified Organisms (GMOs). Our ancestors understood the importance of soil quality in growing hardy and nutritious plants. The seeds of a plant, the life a plant can give, can *never* be healthier than the plant itself; therefore, the health of the seed, of the plant, determines the vitality and nutrients a plant can potentially pass on to its offspring, or the person or animal, that eats the plant. Genetically modified organisms are different from hybrid plants. Hybridized plants are created when two different species reproduce (or are forced to reproduce) together. This creates a new plant with characteristics that blend the characteristics of the two parent plants. For instance, a nectarine is a cross between a peach and a plum.

Genetically modified organisms have DNA that is different from *both* parents. Nature does not make the decision when compiling and interpreting the DNA; instead, a scientist can add, delete, or change a part of the seed's DNA to suit certain purposes. For example, companies have created redder tomatoes, apples that don't brown, and fish that grow to adulthood in half the normal time. Genes and DNA naturally change and evolve gradually over time. As mentioned earlier, the genes of humans have virtually not changed at all in 5,000 years. In genetically modifying a plant or animal, the scientist (or company) can make changes that would *never* occur in nature or that would take tens or hundreds of years to occur naturally. This is good only if the consumer is evolving just as quickly to be able to digest the food and actually derive nutrients from the food. Many genetically modified organisms like corn, soybeans, and beets are genetically modified to be resistant to pesticides or herbicides. Roundup is the most notable example on the market. Not only is the food you are eating now resistant to chemicals, it is also sprayed with them and derives nutrients from soil that is laced with Roundup or other chemicals. The most prevalent GMO crops include corn, soybeans, rice, sugar (beets), canola, alfalfa, potatoes, papaya, zucchini, yellow squash, cotton, and, of course, any animals fed GMO feed. To summarize, GMOs should be avoided for four major reasons.

1. We have not evolved with the plant or animal to be able to digest it. Most likely we never will evolve to be able to digest GMOs, because the DNA changes that scientists and firms choose would never occur in nature.
2. GMOs are typically created to be resistant to certain chemicals. Those same chemicals are "fed" to the plant and create the plant and everything we would potentially eat from the plant. What the plant eats, we eat. Plants and animals can only provide as much nutritional value as they themselves have—the stronger and healthier the plant, the more nutrients for the consumer.
3. The research on the impact of GMOs on animals and humans is split down the middle. The research factor that determines whether or not GMOs are considered "safe" for human consumption seems to be which group *paid* for the research. The studies claiming GMOs are not safe all point to the same factor: erosion of the intestinal cell wall. Not surprisingly, this is how the GMO crop kills insects—it eats through the insects' intestines. One study found that mice fed GMO soy experienced a wide range of emotional problems as well as having extreme difficulty reproducing. The offspring that did survive were sterile.[6]
4. From a vibrational perspective, GMOs test negatively for everyone in my family. They are not good for humans, or animals, to consume. Ultimately, this is all I need to know.

* * *

Organic versus Conventional Foods. Organic foods are the "normal" foods of our grandparents. Similar to GMO products, one of the biggest downfalls of conventional or "nonorganic" plants is that they soak up and eat all of the chemicals and heavy metals that are poured or sprayed on them for various reasons. All of those chemicals and heavy metals are in the plant's makeup when we eat it. Animals and the meat industry are even worse, because the animals are injected with antibiotics and growth hormones to increase yields and shorten growth times. All of these innovations mean lower costs in the food industry, which show up as lower costs for consumers, but the quality degradation has created products that are questionably edible and questionably digestible.

Just because we physically can eat something does not mean we *should.* Any price reduction when we consume these low-quality products is followed by a low quality of life and high health care costs down the road. I consider eating organic food an investment in my family's health that pays off in vitality and not mere survival. Furthermore, organic food contains more nutrients and fewer heavy metals and chemicals than conventional foods.

Good substitutes for organic foods are becoming more and more prevalent as the benefits to our grandparents' foods are being rediscovered and the price of the organic certification stays the same. Because the cost of becoming organically certified or USDA organic can be high, some smaller and more local farmers advertise under the phrase "sustainable farming practices" or "permaculture." Though these sources are not independently verified by a third party like "USDA organic," some research into their practices may give the consumer enough information to make an informed purchase decision. Initially, someone on the standard American diet may not be able to distinguish between organic and conventional foods in a blind taste test. This does not mean there is no difference; it means the body is bogged down with toxins of some kind and lacks awareness. As people progress through the Equilibrium Diet, they will find that conventional foods do not taste as good, or taste bad, or in the cases of some foods, like bananas, which are heavily fumigated, make them physically sick. This is normal and will happen gradually over years on the Equilibrium Diet.

* * *

Organ Meats. The organ meats were the choice cuts for most of our ancestors. Our ancient family members used every part of the animal or fish that they possibly could. This is one of the best sources of foods and nutrients to get the biggest bang for your buck. Given that digestion costs a certain amount of enzymes, or just energy from the body, organ meats offer probably the largest return on investment the body can make. Given the cost of the digestive process, organ meats are intensely rich in vitamins and minerals that are in an easily absorbable form. The human body can easily get a *lot* of nutrients from organ meats with relatively little stress on the digestive system. These were the foods known to build strong and healthy people. Some people shy away from organ meats because of the toxic load organs are assumed to carry, even in organic products. This may be a decent assumption if the meat came from "old" chickens, cattle, and so on. However, we don't eat cows or sheep or chickens that are ten years old or even five years old. Most animals go to slaughter at around twelve to eighteen months of age, which doesn't allow much time to accumulate toxins. Also, organic meats should be exposed to minimal toxic loads for the short time they are alive.

I find that having multiple organ meats ground and mixed (kidney, heart, and liver) seems to provide the best texture and taste for blending into other beef dishes. (See www.equilibriumdiet.com for recipe ideas.)

* * *

Pork. Pork is the most difficult of all meats and proteins to break down. The amino acid strand comprising a pork molecule is the longest of all animal proteins, and many religions abstain from eating it. Our ancestors only ate cured pork, and it was always accompanied by a fermented vegetable product like sauerkraut. The enzyme and probiotic-rich sauerkraut most likely aided the body in breaking down the long amino acid chain. Modern dieters whose direct ancestors thrived on pork can probably handle small amounts. I personally cannot digest pork, but listen to your own body and intuition in deciding whether or not to eat it.

* * *

Sugar. There are countless studies and books written on the negative health impacts of sugar, corn syrup, and related products. Overall, sugar lowers immunity by slowing the effectiveness of white blood cells. Even small amounts of sugar in the diet will reduce the killing power of white blood cells by 50–75 percent (i.e., if the white blood cells were killing one hundred viruses in five minutes before eating a small amount of sugar, then only twenty-five to fifty viruses would be killed in the next five minutes after the sugar was consumed). This effect is found to be immediate upon sugar consumption and lasts for hours after consumption.[7]

Sugar is extremely hard on our adrenal glands, which regulate the body's response to stress. When sugar is consumed, the blood sugar level spikes for a short time. Then the blood sugar level plummets once the glucose is used. This dip in blood sugar is stressful to the body because low blood sugar can be life threatening; therefore, the adrenal cortex attempts to combat the drop by producing cortisol—the stress hormone. In economic terms, this cortisol is relatively expensive to produce (it takes a lot of energy and nutrients), so with repetition, the adrenals' supply dwindles, and adrenal burnout occurs when the nutrients are not properly restored.

Our ancient ancestors did not eat sugar; they consumed only fruits, the sweetest being dates or figs. Some tribes would have consumed small amounts of maple syrup or honey, but even these are not good for anyone with health problems and would have been avoided during times of illness. In my own detox experience since 2010, I have found sugar to be incredibly hard on the body, particularly the liver and the immune system. I eat virtually no sugar, but when I have had small to moderate amounts (the equivalent of three vegan cookies), I found that I instantly needed more sleep, was more tired, and felt like I had a constant hangover. I craved more sugary things later in the day, because my blood sugar would spike and then plummet once the glucose was gone.

After adopting the Equilibrium Diet for three to six months, most people will find that they will not be able to handle much, if any, cane sugar, corn syrup, or other high glycemic sweeteners. This is a result of the body returning to health and working efficiently. People following the diet will be more sensitive to changes anywhere in the body and will notice the feelings associated with the spike in blood sugar that is created by sugar consumption. This may include a tingling or pins-and-needles sensation in the arms, legs, hands, and feet. They may notice that their heart starts racing, or they may feel much more irritable; some people begin to have an almost allergic reaction to sugar with a scratchy throat or increased mucus and congestion. Because sugar reduces the immune system's efficiency for three to five hours after consumption, all of these feelings are to be expected. Sweeteners like agave, xylitol, and molasses do not enter the bloodstream as quickly, so many of these side effects are avoided.

* * *

Artificial Sweeteners like Sweet and Low, Equal, and Splenda. Artificial sweeteners are *artificial*—chemically made by man—and typically contain saccharin, sucralose, or aspartame. Consuming artificial sweeteners increases the toxic load placed on the body, which the liver must detoxify. People ingesting artificial sweeteners are ingesting chemicals that are poisonous to the body. Humans have not evolved to be able to ingest chemicals and man-made substances in a beneficial way—and we probably *never* will.

* * *

Microwaved and Irradiated Foods. I used the microwave nearly every day for something in 2010. If asked about its safety, I would have thought it was perfectly safe and thought it a splendid modern convenience. I knew that microwaves emitted powerful frequencies to "zap" the liquid in food, making the liquid, and hence the food, hot. I also knew that the powerful frequencies were not good to stand in front of, or near, for long periods of time, if at all, but I never related those microwaves with altering the quality of the food being heated. Microwaves are a form of radiation—yes, radiation—like those toxic waves used in radiation therapy to shrink or kill cancerous tumors. Microwaves and irradiation kill everything alive in anything, including food. The molecular structure of the cells in the food is physically changed when irradiated. Enzymes are completely destroyed, and all vitamins and minerals are altered.

This effect is not visible to the naked eye, but you can prove it to yourself using just water. This is a common science fair experiment to show the impact of radiation. Get two identical plants and boil two different sets of water (enough for a week's worth of watering). Boil one on the stove in a stainless steel pan and the other in the microwave. Let the water cool and then give equal amounts of water to your plants. Water as you normally would for the plant type and note the changes. After seven to fourteen days, depending on the frequency of watering and plant size, your stovetop plant will be normal, and your microwaved-water plant will be dead or dying. Microwaved foods do not provide absorbable or bioavailable nutrients to the body. The vibration of the food is changed in such a way that the body considers it toxic material and wants to push it out. Throwing away the microwave is one of the best things a person can do to increase the amount of nutrients (vitamins, minerals, and amino acids) available for absorption for him and his family. I am not recommending cooking every meal from scratch or never eating leftovers—simply heat everything up in a toaster oven, in the oven, or on the stove. As you can see from the houseplant experiment, even boiling water in the microwave for tea is not a good idea—unless you want to end up like the dying houseplant.

As we get healthier and healthier, Equilibrium Dieters will find that microwaved foods send them running for the bathroom an hour or so later with diarrhea. This is a healthy body's reaction to something that has been ingested that is not fit to eat; the liver and body are saying, "Get this toxic material out of here; this is bad stuff." Some people get nauseous, but most seem to pass the toxic material through the bowels. Interestingly, some of the first signs of mild radiation poisoning are gastrointestinal effects like nausea, vomiting, and diarrhea. This is even worse for pregnant women, because what Mama gets—baby gets.

* * *

Sodium is the most important mineral in the body. Other minerals, particularly potassium, cannot even be absorbed when the body's sodium levels are low. Sodium, in the form of raw, unrefined sea salt, is vital to pristine health. The Price Foundation estimates that our ancestors consumed three teaspoons per day of sea salt. Bringing the sodium levels back into balance can go a long way in eliminating headaches, sinusitis, allergies, muscle spasms, twitching, and constipation. Once the body has sufficient sodium, it can work to rebalance its other minerals. I begin each day by drinking one teaspoon of unrefined sea salt, dissolved in a small glass of water. I find drinking the salt dissolved in water makes it much more effective in the body, because the body does not have to go pull moisture from elsewhere to balance and carry the salt to the various cells. If you perspire a lot or are in a warm climate, you may need to drink another glass at midday or before bed. (Note: This is *not* recommended for people with preexisting kidney problems. For these individuals, focus on diet and cleansing to bring your kidneys back into balance first.)

* * *

Phytic Acid and Nuts, Beans, and Grains. I have mentioned phytic acid several times before, but it requires a section of its own for proper explanation. Phytic acid is a chelator, which means that it binds to minerals in the body as it is processed. In this case, each phytic acid molecule *must* bind to eight different mineral molecules before it can be passed through the body. This means that for each molecule of phytic acid we consume, eight different mineral molecules must be taken from somewhere in the body and bonded to the phytic acid for it to be eliminated. Phytic acid does not usually bind to the heavy metals (the stuff we want out of our systems); instead it grabs what is most available with particular attractions to zinc, iron, and calcium. Because it is a chelator, this is sort of like a magnetic attraction—the phytic acid will draw the minerals out of the body from wherever they are—the small intestine, the tendons, the bones, the teeth. Phytic acid *will* bind to eight mineral molecules—that's eight mineral molecules we lose for every molecule of phytic acid we consume. This would not be a big deal if we only consumed phytic acid once in a while—but we don't; most of us consume phytic acid in almost *every* meal.

The phytic acid in improperly prepared nuts, seeds, legumes, beans, rice and grains is draining us of our already scarce mineral levels. The irony of phytic acid is that many people eat "whole grains" to try to be healthier, but whole grains are packed full of these mineral-leeching molecules whereas the refined counterparts: white wheat flour, white rice, and processed white pastas are completely devoid of nutrients *and* devoid of almost all phytic acid as well. This is an unintuitive case; the whole plant products (whole grains) are actually *worse* for us than their processed counterparts. We aren't getting minerals out of either source, but at least with white rice and flour, we aren't being stripped of the minerals we currently have. This took me years of detox and research to learn. I only realized the extent phytic acid plays in our demineralization after I had been eating healthy for over five years and was still zinc deficient. I started wondering, "How long does it take to detox from phytic acid?" And that is when I realized I was still eating it in virtually every meal.

The best research on phytic acid that I have found is by the Weston A. Price Foundation. They have found that oats, rice, corn, and millet have the highest levels of phytic acid and the least amount of phytase of the gluten-free grains. Phytase levels are important because during the fermentation process, phytase is what actually breaks down the phytic acid. Grains like sorghum, amaranth, and teff have some phytase of their own. So—what to do? I am still experimenting, but I have found that the best way to be able to still eat these grains is to soak them in an acidic medium with some phytase-rich buckwheat flour for at least twenty-four hours. I made my own gluten-free sourdough starter that I use to make bread, cornbread, pizza, pancakes, and waffles. Using my sourdough starter (directions can be found at www.equilibriumdiet.com), I simply prepare the flour portion of my recipe in the morning and let it sit, ferment, and rise during the day, and then I bake or cook it for dinner that evening. Allowing the recipe to sit and rise during the day ensures all of the phytic acid is eliminated and that the nutrients in the grains are actually made available to the body. These foods taste so good and are comfort foods that truly strengthen the body.

For nuts and seeds, soaking and sprouting and then roasting provides some benefit, but I have not found any research to quantify how much. Personally, I try to minimize how much of these my family eats, and when we do eat them, we include at least two to three sources of raw calcium as well. So refried beans with loads of raw cheese and a glass of raw goat's milk and blackstrap molasses. This is purely precautionary—I am attempting to flood the body with minerals so the phytic acid can bind to the other minerals in the meal instead of stripping the body. Granted, we aren't getting as many minerals ourselves, but at least we are not being further depleted.

Chocolate, cacao, and coffee also come from beans and contain phytic acid. Chocolate and cacao are interesting because they are actually fermented for around seven days after being harvested. Cacao is touted as a super-food by the nutrition industry, having high levels of magnesium and iron. I have not been able to find any research on the phytic acid and phytase levels in cacao before and after this fermentation process or the actual bioavailability of the minerals. My intuitive guess is that cacao lacks phytase, so even after it is fermented, the phytic acid level remains unchanged, and the minerals are not in an absorbable form. This would explain why many migraine sufferers are triggered by chocolate; the phytic acid is stripping the body, the brain, of minerals. I have already mentioned that many migraines can be eliminated simply by supplementing with sea salt water; minimizing phytic acid from all sources is another remedy. I encourage you to test this. Eliminate all phytic acid sources, including coffee, chocolate, and cacao, for at least ninety days and get your mineral stores up really high. Then, and only then, try a cup of homemade hot chocolate or chocolate milk made with coconut milk and raw cacao and see how you feel.

Phytic acid is a big deal. It has been silently leeching our minerals for decades now, draining us of our life force. It is an even bigger deal for children who are growing and developing and need all the minerals possible to create a strong skeleton and brain. In general, more minerals means we suffer less line loss, and we can carry more voltage—we are more powerful, and we have more energy in every way imaginable. When our mineral levels are high, we feel great.

CHAPTER 18

The Low-Down on Other Diets

We must learn what we *are not* in order to learn what we *are*. A large part of developing the Equilibrium Diet was observing what *didn't* work in existing diets. A larger part was identifying health and recreating its conditions. This is a very different strategy than trying to eliminate disease—yet eliminating disease is a by-product of eating efficiently. There are some good diet recommendations on the market for particular situations; however, each of these diets was created with symptom alleviation in mind. This means the diet's inventor had an idea of what they wanted to *avoid*—this results in an *overcorrection*. Instead of bringing the body back into balance, these diets bring the body away from the symptom and then to some overcorrected point. In the raw food diet, this overcorrection is marked by bad teeth. The Paleo diet is marked by liver stress, hunger, and the overconsumption of protein. In this chapter, I summarize various mainstream diets and the benefits and costs of each. Most of the diets simply don't yield vibrant health and energy because the inputs and processes are inferior. Poor quality manifests as liver congestion, acidosis, and vitamin and mineral deficiencies; each of these general imbalances causes a host of other problems.

The liver is the chemical factory and the lifeline of the body; we are only as healthy as our livers. Given the time and resources to produce and clean, the liver ensures that hormones are regulated and that the immune system destroys all harmful invaders—we only get sick when the liver is overburdened. To put this in business terms, we get sick when our liver is the bottleneck. If we are taking in more wastes and toxins than the liver can handle, the liver works at maximum capacity, and we experience the toxins that the liver hasn't gotten to yet; this is *dis-ease*—I call this *liver congestion*.

When the liver is congested, it is backed up like rush-hour traffic on a freeway: we have to wait out the consequences. To make matters worse, if we keep adding more toxins to the liver's load, the liver is never able to catch up, and we must live with the consequences: headaches, fatigue, bad breath, hangover-type feelings, and moodiness. As the congestion worsens, the liver recruits help to try to eliminate the debris—the help comes in the form of viruses, bacteria, parasites, and yeasts like *Candida albicans*. These critters eat the by-products of all the toxins and waste putrefying in the body that the liver has not had time to neutralize and remove. The critters come with a host of baggage when they establish themselves in a person's body: fatigue, reduced attention span and mental clarity, hormonal disruptions, skin problems, intestinal problems, gas, and absorption problems (because the critters are typically growing out of the intestinal wall, creating a leaky gut).

Healing and vibrant health are possible only when the liver can handle the entire toxic load it faces—plus repair any areas in need of some TLC. My goal in designing the Equilibrium Diet was to minimize the burden on the liver, conditional on obtaining nutrients to sustain health and energy levels. Given that we must eat to provide the liver with the building blocks it needs to repair and regenerate new cells, we want to provide the inputs at the absolute lowest cost to the liver. In minimizing the costs the liver bears, we free it up to heal old wounds and clean out the body. Over time, this means a stronger immune system, more nutrients are absorbed from food, hormones are regulated, inflammation ceases to exist, and parasites, viruses, candida, and bacteria cannot live in an environment without food—our accumulated waste creates their buffet. A body without disease is a body without waste.

* * *

Raw or "Living" Food diets provide the opportunity for more and higher quality nutrients than most other diets; however, diets consisting largely of raw foods are unsustainable in the long run for most people, because the diets encourage "eating for summer" year-round. Raw foods are great for summer because they are cooling to the body and provide lots of vitamins and electrolytes (minerals), which are easily destroyed in cooking. The electrolytes usually end up in the cooking water and are thrown out if the water isn't consumed with the veggies.

Raw foods are great for a cleanse, and I recommend eating as many living foods as you can when you first start cleansing—unless it is the dead of winter—but in the long run, eating only raw food taxes the body. It takes more digestive activity to break down raw foods than lightly cooked foods. Many of us cannot actually break down raw foods at all, because vegetables have tough cell walls called cellulose. Light cooking for most vegetables is important, because the heat breaks down those tough cell walls (so does freezing them). In general, the vast majority of foods eaten should be predigested (either through cooking or with acids like lemon and raw apple cider vinegar) to minimize the stress on the body. The less energy the body has to spend wringing nutrients out of foods, the more energy it can spend using those nutrients to repair the body.

Even in the best raw food and living food diets where the vast majority of vegetables are predigested in some way, the foods tend to be cooling. This reduces heat in the body, which is great in summertime but miserable during a cold winter. This is particularly acute in older people, children (who are still building their nutrient base), new mothers (particularly the first six weeks after the baby is born), and individuals who fit the *vata* constitution in Ayurvedic medicine.[1]

Raw foods, whether predigested or not, still require high levels of stomach acid and enzymes to be properly broken down for the body to receive nutrients. Most Americans lack the enzymes and stomach acidity to properly digest raw foods. Eating a raw foods diet when one cannot properly digest the food will deplete the body of nutrients as existing stores are used. As the body's nutrients, particularly mineral stores, dwindle, the organs and skeletal systems weaken as the body leaches the minerals it needs for day-to-day operations from mineral-rich areas. Raw foodies often have dental problems, like worn tooth enamel and cavities. Simply put, it is incredibly difficult, if not impossible, to get all of the minerals we need for health from raw food alone. Our soils today are much more depleted than they were in our grandparents' era; even organic produce lacks the mineral content that our grandparents' conventional food had. Perhaps this is due to the limits and constraints of our digestive system. Perhaps we physically cannot eat enough plant material *and* digest it to maintain vibrant health—the animal sources give us the highest return on the cost or investment of digestion. This is like choosing between two investments that *both* yield $500. The first requires a $1000 investment and guarantees a 50 percent return; the second requires a $10,000 investment and guarantees a 5 percent return. You end up making $500 in either case, but the second opportunity requires a lot more to get the deal done.

Furthermore, even relatively healthy individuals who embark on the raw or living foods diet can find themselves lightheaded, dizzy, or with blackouts. This is primarily due to the timing of when certain types of food are eaten. Raw and living foodies do not attempt to work with the pH cycle of the body by loading up on proteins early in the day. Because these dieters still consume the vast majority of their protein at night, they will not absorb as much of the protein—and their livers are working harder during those nighttime hours. In the long run, this taxes the immune system by putting excess stress on the liver and depletes the body's existing stores of protein, because the liver is forced to make more and more amino acids.

I am a huge advocate for whole foods and would love to promote raw food, but I simply have not seen any data to support that a raw food lifestyle is the way to obtain pristine health for a lifetime. All of the data seem to support a diet high in lightly cooked vegetables, raw dairy products, soaked and roasted nuts and seeds, seafood, and organ meat. The foods that should be eaten raw are milk, cheese and butter, fruits, and even some meats and fish. The following lists are included to help you determine whether or not raw foods are good for you.

Signs Raw Vegetables Are Good for You:
1. You crave salads and other raw vegetables.
2. You feel satisfied for at least four hours after having a meal consisting of largely raw vegetables.
3. You feel tired after a meal of largely cooked vegetables.

Signs Raw Vegetables Are Not Good for You:
1. You crave cooked vegetables or warm foods or feel like you have to *make* yourself eat salads.
2. You feel hungry one to three hours after eating a meal consisting largely of raw foods. (This is a sign you are not getting many nutrients out of the raw vegetables and your body is looking for more.)

3.	You do not feel tired after a meal of largely cooked vegetables.
4.	You observe undigested raw food in your stool.

To recap, consuming mostly raw foods is *not* beneficial for the vast majority of people for several reasons:

1. Cellulose (in raw plants) is very tough to break down.
2. Our ancestors did not eat many vegetables raw.
3. Most people do not have enough stomach acid to properly digest raw food. This is exacerbated when proteins are consumed after 2:00 p.m. and sugars before 2:00 p.m., because the body tries to remain acidic at all times. This acidosis leads to malabsorption and disease.
4. Raw foods are very cooling to the body. This is good in times of heat but crippling in times of cold weather.

Summary of imbalances: low protein absorption; taxes pancreas (which produces enzymes); cooling to the body's energy system; weak immune system in long run as body's stores of nutrients are depleted; skeletal and dental problems.

* * *

The Pro-Vita diet is similar to the raw and living foods diets, but it does work with the pH cycle of the body, and it allows for dairy and meat. This eliminates almost all of the problems with raw and living foods diets (liver congestion, low protein absorption). But the Pro-Vita diet still recommends large amounts of raw food and "eats for summer" year-round. As mentioned earlier, the raw foods are difficult to digest, especially for people who lack sufficient stomach acid, and even for our primitive ancestors with robust digestive systems. Furthermore, the cycles of the year, and our lives, that require additional heat are not accounted for in the Pro-Vita diet.

Summary of imbalances: taxing on pancreas (which produces enzymes); cooling to the body's energy system; dairy and improperly prepared wheat are inflammatory; weak immune system in long run as body's stores of nutrients are depleted from a largely raw diet.

* * *

Vegan. Because the vegan diet does not allow for the consumption of any animal products, it does reduce the liver's stress level and some liver congestion; however, a vegan diet cannot sustain a healthy body for most people. All primitive societies ate small amounts of meat and large amounts of fat. A diet lacking animal products makes it very difficult to obtain iron, vitamin B-12, and vitamin D (as well as the other fat-soluble vitamins: A, E, K, and F). Vitamin B-12 is only found in animal products and some sea algae. Although there is more iron in chocolate (as a percentage) than red meat, iron in chocolate is virtually impossible to absorb—the iron in red meat is *heme* iron, which is the most bioavailable—the most easily absorbed form. Because of the poor variety of fat-soluble vitamins consumed by vegans, they may suffer all the consequences of a diet low in protein and fat: primarily skin problems and a weak immune system. Vegans are prone to dizziness and blackouts, because protein is still consumed in larger quantities in the evening.

Summary of imbalances: liver congestion, anemia, low mineral reserves, fatigue, dizziness, susceptible to viruses/colds/flus, skin and hair problems, improperly prepared wheat is inflammatory and demineralizing.

I would also like to address veganism and vegetarianism from a spiritual perspective, because many "spiritual" authors cite a diet free from animal products as necessary for spiritual growth and enlightenment. Among others, Rudolf Steiner talks about the taxing effects of meat on the body in his book, *Nutrition* and Andreas Moritz recommends a vegetarian diet in *The Amazing Liver and Gallbladder Flush*. In my experience, this recommendation is based on two misunderstood concepts: the pH cycle of the body and eliminating the desire for animal products. Spiritual seekers see the benefits of avoiding meat at night and associate it with avoiding meat all the time—this is based on avoiding the liver congestion that is always created when meat is consumed at night, or after 2:00 p.m. No current studies exist comparing vegetarians or vegans to people who eat meat only before 2:00 p.m.; however, we can look to the primitive tribes documented by Weston A. Price, DDS, which showed the leading factor in robust health was the lack of sugar, refined and processed food, and the inclusion of organ meat, seafood, and raw milk products. I hypothesize that if a modern study were to be undertaken, it would conclude that people eating meat (and mostly organ meats) before 2:00 p.m. are much healthier than their vegan and vegetarian counterparts.

In pursuing a vegan, vegetarian, or raw-food diet, many seekers are able to avoid the liver congestion and weakened immune system that occurs when meats are consumed after 2:00 p.m. In the short run, this can lead to more energy and reduced inflammation and disease, because the liver is able to function more efficiently; however, in the long run, without adequately replacing the liver's supply of amino acids, vitamins, and minerals, the body will become more and more depleted as the needed nutrients are leached from the organs and skeletal system. Teeth problems, brittle hair, weakened bones, and weak reproduction follow. These spiritual seekers are reducing their liver congestion but giving up large amounts of vitamins and minerals when they do not consume meat—specifically, organ meat and seafood before 2:00 p.m. and raw milk. This tradeoff does not have to happen; just eat the meats before 2:00 p.m., and we negate the liver congestion and retain the easily absorbable vitamins, minerals, and fats.

Some vegans make the argument against animal cruelty, even in the cases of organic and free-range meat, because of the way the USDA classifies the two, and I sympathize with this, but instead of jeopardizing my health, along with the animals, I order organ meats from local organic farmers and work toward having my own animals. We cannot change the world, or ourselves, if we are exhausted from vitamin and mineral deficiencies. Thanks to the local foods movement, it is becoming easier and easier to find someone, even a neighbor, who keeps chickens or goats or rabbits. In buying from them, you support yourself and the loving treatment of the animal community.

In regards to eliminating the desire for animal products, spiritual seekers have confused a *by-product* of spirituality with something needed to *obtain* spirituality. Spiritual seekers eliminate animal products from their diets thinking it will bring enlightenment, because they observe gurus and yogis avoiding animal products and sometimes all food. These same seekers often have intense cravings for animal products—particularly red meat. The desire for animal products falls away naturally as we advance in health and spirituality. It is not an internal battle or even a choice; one day, we simply wake up and have no desire for meat. Eventually, our desire for all animal products simply falls away; however, this can only happen once the body is healthy enough and operating efficiently enough to recycle current stores *and* utilize plant products. This can happen only when *robust* nutritional solvency is obtained. Any craving for animal products before this point represents instinctual urges from the body to get nutrients in an easily absorbable form—ignoring the urge compromises the nutrition integrity of the body.

* * *

A **macrobiotic diet** is a form of vegetarianism; however, macrobiotic dieters cook all of their foods and avoid virtually all fats. Essentially, the macrobiotic diet does a pretty good job of minimizing all costs of digestion; however, it doesn't provide large amounts of usable nutrients to the body. Macrobiotic diets can be good in the short run for people who are so diseased—so nutritionally bankrupt—that they have virtually no digestive energy left of their own. Meats, particularly when consumed at night, are particularly stressful on the liver and body, so macrobiotic dieters avoid this stress much like the other vegetarians. In the long run, the macrobiotic diet is low in the protein, minerals, and fats needed for long-term health.

Summary of imbalances: low vitamin and mineral intake and absorption, fatigue, dizziness, susceptibility to viruses/colds/flus, skin and hair problems (improperly prepared wheat is inflammatory and demineralizing).

* * *

Low-fat or no-fat diets rarely limit much except for fat and sometimes sugar consumption. Extreme low-fat diets are often recommended by doctors in cases of gallbladder problems to minimize the discomfort, usually in conjunction with antinausea and pain medications. All of these "remedies" address the symptom of gallbladder malfunction but not the underlying issue creating the problem: nutritional bankruptcy and liver congestion. The symptom is a red flag saying, "Hi! Look at me! Something is out of balance, and I'm your clue to discover what it is if you just pay attention." Often these diets recommend no-fat or low-fat cheeses, cream cheeses, milks, ice creams, and so on. Processed and refined foods are still consumed. When fat is removed, something must be added to replace the flavor; usually this is refined salt, MSG (monosodium glutamate), sugar, or other preservatives, so low-fat diets add preservatives and chemicals back into the diet. Furthermore, because fat consumption is restricted, all of the vitamins and minerals that require fats to be properly absorbed (particularly vitamins A, E, D, and K) will not be available to the body. For vitamins A, E, D, and K, sufficient fats must be present for the body to be able to use the vitamins, and intuitively, often the best source of the vitamins is the fat itself—seal oil is one of the richest sources of vitamin A; raw pastured butter contains all of the fat-soluble vitamins in addition to vitamin X. (Vitamin X was discovered by Weston A. Price and is an activator for the absorption of many other vitamins and minerals.)

Low-fat diets are typically laden with inflammatory and processed foods like wheat, dairy, and other refined products. These products last for a long time on store shelves but provide virtually zero nutritional value in a usable form. People on such diets will consume inflammatory products and eat away at their body's existing stores of fat-soluble vitamins (if they have any). The adrenal glands will deplete because of the high levels of inflammation. The immune system will gradually weaken, and fatigue and disease will set in. As with other standard American diets, liver congestion will be rampant because of eating processed foods and eating proteins at night.

Summary of imbalances: liver congestion; inability to absorb nutrients; fatigue, disease, and compromised immune system; risk of all diseases associated with standard American diet, including acidosis, heart disease, gallbladder problems, high blood pressure, high cholesterol, diabetes, and candida overgrowth.

* * *

The Paleo diet recommends eating "like cavemen" with minimal processed and refined foods. This is similar to the Equilibrium Diet with two major exceptions: excessive amounts of protein (particularly meat) are consumed at the wrong time of day—dinnertime—and all grains are avoided. This generates all of the liver stress and congestion of the standard American diet but without preservatives. The preservatives and refined foods are eliminated, which represents a huge leap toward health, and overall inflammation will decrease; however, the body will never get enough time to heal and cleanse until the proteins are avoided at night. Avoiding grains, if they are improperly prepared, could theoretically reduce phytic acid consumption; however, Paleo does allow nuts and seeds, which are also high in phytic acid (soaking nuts and seeds does not completely eliminate it).

The most common complaint I hear from people on the Paleo diet is, "I never feel full or satisfied; I eat a steak and a pork chop for dinner, and I'm still hungry." This is because the body *is* still hungry for nutrients. It is incredibly costly to the body to digest large amounts of protein at night, and we get very little energy from them because the body is in the alkaline phase of the pH cycle. Most of these people are eating fruit for breakfast, which automatically spikes the blood sugar and creates a blood sugar "crash" an hour or so later. If the Paleo dieters would just have the steak and pork chop for breakfast and the fruit for dinner, they would feel much more satisfied, have more energy, and strengthen their immune systems.

Summary of imbalances: liver congestion, too much protein at night, hunger, reduced immunity to disease, possible demineralization from phytic acid in nuts and seeds.

* * *

The anti-candida diet is slightly healthier than the Atkins diet because it strives to eliminate all sources of sugar, even most fruits. It does recommend eliminating processed food and caffeine as well, but its focus is on consuming large amounts of protein. The anti-candida diet can help with candida-related problems in the short run; however, participants will hit a plateau that cannot be crossed until the liver is given time to rest—which happens when protein consumption occurs in the morning and is avoided after 2:00 p.m.

Summary of imbalances: low protein, extreme liver congestion and stress, risk of all diseases associated with liver congestion, including acidosis, heart disease, gallbladder problems, high blood pressure, high cholesterol, diabetes, and candida overgrowth.

* * *

Nourishing Traditions, based largely on the research by Weston A. Price, DDS, in *Nutrition and Physical Degeneration*, does the best job of integrating the primitive food selections and modern life. It eliminates processed and refined food and most sources of sugar. The lifestyle also tends to emphasize the need for evolving food choices as the seasons and geographic location change. Nourishing Traditions recommends eating dairy products, particularly raw milk, cheese, and butter. It also advocates eating small amounts of raw meat, because most primitive societies were found to eat at least some portion of their meat (or seafood) raw. Nourishing Traditions is similar to the Paleo diet in that it eliminates all foods not eaten by primitive people and focuses on meats. The Nourishing Traditions diet does a better job of cooking and preparing food in the ancient ways, which makes the nutrients more bioavailable for digestion. This includes sprouting (or at least soaking) all grains like wheat, spelt, rice, and corn. It includes eating lots of fats and fermented foods like sauerkraut, pickles, and kimchi with every meal. The fermenting process adds back beneficial enzymes and bacteria that aid in the digestive process, and the fats provide a host of fat-soluble vitamins and activators. The diet emphasizes the importance of vitamins and minerals found in organ meats, bone broths, and raw dairy.

Nourishing Traditions neglects to account for the pH cycle of the body and as a result recommends consuming meats and proteins at night. This coupled with the potentially large amounts of cow's milk products (even when raw) present the largest health risks of the diet: liver congestion, reduced immunity to disease, and inflammation from dairy products. Because the vast majority of protein is consumed at night in this diet, the follower is subject to low protein absorption and liver congestion.

Summary of imbalances: low protein, liver congestion and stress, inflammation from dairy and wheat products, reduced immunity to disease.

* * *

The mini-meal diet. Some diets recommend eating four to six "small" meals per day. Sometimes this is used to stabilize blood sugar in the case of diabetes or hypoglycemia; however, such advice treats the symptom of the problem instead of the root cause. Blood sugar is "managed" by propping it up throughout the day; however, managing blood sugar by eating four to six meals per day is incredibly costly to the body in terms of energy, enzymes, digestive juices, and liver stress. If someone were to eat frequent small meals for years on end, they would end up with pancreas problems because enzyme levels are depleted, and they would display many of the symptoms of liver stress. In this dietary model, the liver is constantly preoccupied with digestion.

I recommend eating two to four meals per day. Following the Equilibrium Diet, the blood sugar naturally stabilizes to an almost perfect flat line because there are no ups and there are no downs—you are like a tractor-trailer truck plowing through the day. Once the body's pH cycle is stabilized, the body is perfectly happy to maintain its acidic-alkaline cycle, which enables the low-cost digestion of protein and carbohydrates at the respective times during the day. The hunger pains and demand for food cease almost entirely. You will know you have found your equilibrium if you eat a breakfast of four to five proteins and are not hungry for a full four and a half to five hours. At the five-hour mark, you should notice that you would be willing to eat again. The same rule would apply after lunch. Usually another meal at lunch of four to five proteins, buffered with vegetables, will be enough to make you too full to eat for the rest of the night. This is normal; your liver has had all it needs for the day and is ready to cleanse early.

Several groups of people who may need the extra meal or two include athletes, pregnant and breastfeeding women, children, and those who are severely nutrient-depleted. For all meals, the cost-benefit analysis is a must. We should ask ourselves the following questions. (When at a party or eating out, sometimes answering these questions means I am better off not eating than consuming foods that lower my vibration.)

1. *Am I really hungry?* Or am I trying to block an emotion?

2. *Do my food choices at least cover the cost of me digesting them?* For instance, processed food, refined flour, and sugar *never* do. Am I getting a positive return on my digestive investment? Because remember, the cost of digesting anything is pretty much the same regardless of what and how much you eat. (The investment must be positive a large percentage of the time to lift us out of nutritional bankruptcy.)

3. *Can I eat enough in this sitting to make digestion worth the cost?* I do not mean stuff yourself, but you should feel full. We don't want to be eating a small amount to just "get by" because "just getting by" is costly to the body.

These three questions are offered as a general guide to begin thinking of digestion as a process that is necessary but *costly* to your body. Thinking about how we answer these questions shows us how we are doing and how we have, or have not, planned our day to take excellent care of our number-one asset: ourselves. As a former hypoglycemic, I learned quickly that I had to set aside a large enough block of time to eat enough food in a relaxed manner at breakfast to maintain my blood sugar. I am much happier, much more relaxed, and have more energy when I eat a large breakfast and lunch as opposed to snacking throughout the day.

* * *

Any of the above diets can be adjusted to evolve into the Equilibrium Diet. As you can see, many of the diets have discovered, or stumbled upon, a part or a subset of the Equilibrium Diet—it is as if we have all been searching for something, some truth, that we know exists, and we find a piece of it here and there, but we have still been missing the big picture. All of these diets are pieces of the puzzle that need to be integrated in order to see that big picture. The big picture is not about weight loss or keeping candida at bay—it is about eating in a way that produces vibrant health for a lifetime for *everyone*. We are all unique, our health needs are unique, and we all begin at a different place in our story of health; for robustness, this implies that we need a framework flexible enough to run the gamut. It needs to work for people who are relatively healthy but looking for the next level of vitality, and for people who have never eaten a salad in their life and suffer from a multitude of health challenges. The Equilibrium Diet is economically, scientifically, and intuitively simple—because of this simplicity, the Equilibrium Diet allows for great flexibility for people in all times and places, from the deserts to the Arctic and from infancy to old age.

You should eat what your ancestors ate. If your ancestors didn't eat it, you shouldn't either. You should also prepare the foods in traditional ways and eat them at traditional times (both time of the year and time of day). And if it grows in your area and climate and the food is ready to eat (fresh) that time of the year, then eat it—if not, don't! The more closely we adhere to these principles, the healthier we will be.

CHAPTER 19

Fear of Getting Healthy

Many of us are afraid of actually taking responsibility for our lives and getting healthy. The three main fears come in the guise of effort, time, and cost. We tell ourselves, "It takes too much effort to learn and do what needs to be done to change my lifestyle." We tell ourselves, "It is too much of a time commitment to do a cleanse *and* choose mental and physical activities that help detox—after all, there are only twenty-four hours in a day." Or, "It is so expensive to eat well—I can't afford it." We tell ourselves these things because we have created a world of denial that makes us *feel* like outside pressures control us. In truth, we choose and create everything. Each of the above statements reflects a deeper fear—the fear of not being worthy of the best at a fundamental level—the only level that matters. We can live in big houses and drive fancy cars, but if we are not investing in our true selves, all of the glitz and glam is overcompensating for the love and nurturing we have not given ourselves.

In all of these fears, we are missing one *major* concept—the healthy future version of us is *very* different from present-day us. We are stuck and thinking of how our world and life *currently* appear; instead, we need to focus on possibility and what we *could* be—this is how we invite transformational change to work its magic through us. For instance, what if instead of needing nine to twelve hours of sleep, your healthy future version only needed six or eight? What if you need only eight hours of work to get done what used to take you ten or eleven hours? It all boils down to efficiency—in getting healthy, we *create* more time; we create more money—when our priorities shift, so does our reality. Here are a few examples of how this is physically supported when we chose to eat well and invest in ourselves.

1. The nutrient density of organic food is higher than non-organic (conventional) food, and the pesticide residue and heavy metals are lower. In terms of bang for our buck, we should be willing to pay more for organic food than conventional, because we are getting more of the good stuff and less of the bad! This makes sense; if you dump chemicals and pesticides on crops, the crops are going to absorb them through the soil and water, and the chemicals are going to end up in the plants. If you feed cattle antibiotics, it's not surprising that the drugs are going to end up inside the cow, and when the cow becomes meat, the antibiotics are in the meat! (Please note that it is typically cheaper to buy organic from organic grocery stores than to buy organic foods from traditional grocery stores.)

2. You eat a lot less when you eat according to the Equilibrium Diet than you do when you do not eat well. Our bodies need nutrients, not chemicals, preservatives, sugar, and GMOs. When the body is fed low-quality foods it digests them and then says, "Hey, I'm hungry; I need actual nutrients here. Give me more food." Low-quality eaters are hungry all the time. Your detox period will be more expensive than your new healthy equilibrium, because you will be cleansing and building the body at fast rates; this requires a lot of nutrients. However, the healthier you get, the less you need to simply maintain your new optimum.

3. You shift away from expensive food—the processed stuff. In turning toward health, we release our need for processed food of all kinds: organic and conventional.

4. You eat out less on the Equilibrium Diet. I suggest not eating out for the first ninety days to provide a strong foundation. After that, you will have mastered what you should and should not eat and have confidence in your choices. Big cities with restaurants that serve whole foods, vegan, vegetarian, and raw foods tend to be a bit easier to navigate but are also going to be more expensive. Fast food (McDonald's, Subway, etc.), Chinese food, and pizza joints are not going to be healthy regardless of your lack of food sensitivities—all of their food, even the salads, are laden with chemicals, additives, fillers, and/or preservatives.

5. Reduced health care expenses and a higher quality of life. How can you put a dollar figure on feeling great? This shows up in not just fewer sick days taken but your smile, your energy, your relationships—your entire life! Even better, as you return to your natural state of vitality, your expenses on Western medicine dwindle—the need for all prescription and OTC medications fall away. Yes, herbal and homeopathic remedies may be substituted but usually at a fraction of the cost, and we actually *feel* good.

6. Reduced spending of money and time in other areas. As we get healthier, our priorities shift, and we become more efficient in all areas of our life. And remember, efficiency isn't all about production; it is about really investing in ourselves and nourishing ourselves, which typically means we make more time for relaxing and doing things we love, because those become the priority as we begin to see the world and ourselves more clearly. I was a coffee and amaretto-sour addict before we started detoxing. Today, I don't spend any time or money at the Starbucks' drive-through or liquor store. Our priorities shift as our health improves; we don't have to *make* ourselves *do* anything—it just happens!

In short, eating organic and healthy foods does not have to be expensive—and it actually saves us money in the long run—but it does require planning. My family spends $1100–$1300 per month on all groceries and food. We rarely eat out, so this represents the total food bill for a family of four. This includes drinking a half gallon of raw goat's milk per day. If the budget is really tight, we could always shift our protein consumption away from the meats and toward the nuts, seeds, and legumes. Organic rice and beans sell for less than three dollars per pound in Greenville, South Carolina, whereas organic ground beef sells for eight dollars and higher per pound; commercial ground beef is about five dollars per pound. By incorporating organ meats, which are usually half the price of muscle meats, we can reduce our overall price per serving of meat too.

Ultimately, if someone still chooses to see eating healthily as expensive, he must ask himself: **"Aren't I worth it? Aren't I worth the best?"** Our physical three-dimensional bodies are the Lamborghinis that carry us around. This is the equivalent of driving around in a Bentley and trying to fill up with the cheapest grade-87 gas you can find, because the grade-93 is "too expensive." This may be a sign that our financial priorities are not in line with our true selves. Our body, our health, is our most valuable asset. When we feel good, when we feel healthy, we enjoy living and *want* to live. No matter what we may feel or think, deep down underneath all of the lies and self-hate that society has tried to program into us, we do love ourselves—a lot! Every single one of us! Now, let's get to work, because the integrity of our cells, and of our life force, is built on what we eat—if we eat low-quality foods and pseudo-foods, we will create a low-quality life experience.

* * *

Questions

1. If you think that eating healthily is expensive, try tracking every single purchase you make for one week, and then for one month. Review your list of purchases at the end of the week and the month.
    a. In doing this, put them into two columns (or write an "E" for ego or an "H" for higher self next to each purchase). Do not overthink this; write down your gut reaction. You may find that certain foods fall under one category or the other.
    b. Next, go through your list of purchases again and write a yes (Y) or no (N) for whether or not that purchase gets you closer to achieving your goals. Be as honest with yourself as you possibly can. There are no right or wrong answers—just notice that the ego is present anytime fear or a negative emotion is the driver behind a purchase. Answering these questions can help you see the program your subconscious is running.

CHAPTER 20

Ninety-Day Program Overview

If you want to become something, act like you already are that thing. We create our reality every day. Think. Act. Be. Be. Act. Become.

If you want to be healthy, act like you are. Choose to eat according to the Equilibrium Diet, and you *will* become healthy. Gradually, your tolerance for chemicals, sugar, chlorinated water, harsh music, and gossip will slip away. You will find that you simply do not desire these anymore; you find them off-putting. After all, why would someone willingly put inferior products into the most valuable car in the universe?

Steps 1–8 are the basic lifestyle steps that you can implement in your life over the next ninety days to practice *being* healthy. After your initial thirty to forty-five days without sugar and processed food, your health will improve dramatically. Supplemental cleanses are also included in the following chapters to help quickly rid your body of toxic material. Please note that you never have to do any of these or *anything*; however, the more you do, the more closely you will replicate my experience and the more quickly you will see results.

1. Abstain from all drugs, cigarettes, tobacco, and alcohol. Abstain from all caffeine. Small amounts of green tea are permissible only because the green tea itself can be great to minimize detox symptoms, especially from heavy metals.
2. Juice fast for a minimum of seven days
3. Master the Equilibrium Diet and avoid tap water.
4. Colon cleanse/parasite cleanse

5. Moderate exercise to get the energy flowing
6. Heavy metal detox (for your brain and nervous system)
7. Detox support
8. Liver and gallbladder flush (for a weak immune system, cholesterol, allergies, and anything else that ails you!)

* * *

Step 1. No drugs or alcohol. The goal with all of the steps is to reduce stress on the liver. Cigarettes, alcohol, and drugs tax the liver and body at incredible rates. If your fear surrounding these "blocks" is so great that you feel you must indulge within the ninety-day program, please consider the following substitutes.

1. **Kava kava** is an herb from the South Pacific that induces relaxation, takes the edge off, and offers many of the effects of alcohol without the liver stress. This can be ordered from Amazon.com or found at most herbal stores.

2. Clear hard alcohols like **organic vodka**. When mixed with mineral water or lemon juice, this is the one alcoholic beverage allowed in moderation. It is permissible on rare occasions because of its extremely low sugar content, though it will stress the liver. Wine is high in sugar and contains sulfites, which are to be avoided. Beer is also very high in sugar and should be avoided entirely during the first ninety days.

3. **Coffee cruda** is a homeopathic remedy that brings on deep and restful sleep without any grogginess in the morning. This is wonderful for adults, children, and even infants. It can be ordered from Amazon.com or found at any store carrying homeopathic remedies. A *melatonin* supplement can also help with sleep problems.

Caffeine is avoided because it pushes everything into the bloodstream more quickly and creates a roller-coaster effect on blood sugar and the adrenal glands. Caffeine is extremely stressful on the adrenals, because the glands try to stabilize the wild cortisol swings induced by caffeine. Substances that carry caffeine (coffee, black tea, chocolate) are all very acidifying to the body, and we are trying to achieve the opposite—an alkaline cellular environment where most harmful organisms (cancer, bacteria, parasites) cannot live. Caffeine addicts may want to take two weeks before beginning the juice fast to gradually work their way off caffeine first. For coffee lovers, some decent substitutes include the following.

1. **DandyBlend** is a gluten-free blend of dandelion, beets, and barley that tastes enough like coffee to satisfy most coffee lovers. It can be ordered on Amazon.com.

2. **Decaf coffee** is not preferred because it is still incredibly acidifying to the body and processed using chemicals.

3. **Teechino** is a blend of almonds, vanilla, and barley and can be purchased at most organic food stores. This is probably the best coffee substitute I have found.

4. **Sparkling water** mixed with **100 percent juice,** or **kombucha** are good substitutes for soft drink and carbonation lovers.

Remember, caffeine is a symptom that our life is out of balance and needs external stimulus to stay awake. Often, we make tradeoffs, so the most important thing for the first ninety days is eliminating all sources of sugar. If you must have your morning coffee, do so, but be sure to add cream (preferably unpasteurized) to help cut down on the coffee's acidity; do *not* use flavored creamers, which are packed with chemicals, sugar, and preservatives. As we become more balanced, we naturally turn away from foods that shift us away from balance. Coffee, caffeine, alcohol, and drugs simply do not appeal to us anymore. I have told my husband *many* times, and many people have told me, "I will never, ever give up this or that or coffee or tea," only to have no desire for that item a few months later. It is okay to be open to our own changing desires.

* * *

Why the Diet and Program Work

The Equilibrium Diet leads to health, rejuvenation, and enlightenment, because it provides maximum nutrients at the lowest possible cost to the body. It is efficient. By using food combinations, cleansing programs, and avoiding proteins past 2:00 p.m., the diet reduces the body's toxic load. Not only is the toxic load minimized, but the effectiveness of the liver is maximized for old toxins to be eliminated. The combination of organ meat, raw milk, and seafood provides the building blocks the body needs to strengthen and rejuvenate, gradually restoring nutritional *solvency*. Working with the body's pH cycle eliminates acidosis, protein toxicity, and protein deficiency. When proteins are eliminated after 2:00 p.m., the liver can clean while you sleep instead of digesting. The fasting and colon and liver cleanses quickly strip the body of years of layers of toxic material, which enables the body to begin operating with a new, cleaner system. This increases nutrient absorption, and as a by-product, we find ourselves wanting much less food. The *quantity* of our food consumption drops so long as the *quality* remains high.

The body uses the food it needs incredibly efficiently—we are getting the maximum return on our digestive investment. Low energy cost and high nutrient absorption imply minimal wastes are generated, and greater levels of equilibrium health are experienced. The Equilibrium Diet combines the nutrient availability of animal proteins with the reduced liver burden associated with vegetarian diets. Literally, it is the best of both worlds: high nutrient availability without putting *any* additional stress on the liver.

CHAPTER 21

Fasting

Fasting is essential, because it creates a clean break between your old food habits and the food habits you will adopt in the Equilibrium Diet. Without the discipline and results of the fast, it is very difficult to have the willpower to adhere to the Equilibrium Diet for ninety days to *indefinitely*. Furthermore, during a fast, you free up the body's energy to "clean house and repair." The body spends around 80 percent of its energy on digestion. During a fast or juice fast, the nutrients are absorbed directly from the small intestine and are not stopped in the stomach to be acted upon by digestive agents. The fast is a fast-track tool used to jolt you away from your current life-state and give you momentum toward health. The clean break with the *old* can give you the strength you need to run the full course of the dietary changes for the next three months. A food fast is similar to a technology fast; that is, taking a break from television, computer, cell phone, and so on. We eliminate the inputs going into the body in order to take inventory and align our own thoughts and lines of communication. We probably don't want to stop eating or communicating with the world forever, but it is rejuvenating to take a break.

While on a juice fast, no solid foods are consumed, only liquids. We are still drinking our full amount of daily calories, but our bodies expend minimal energy to process those nutrients—this frees up enormous stores of energy to be sent around the body to clean and repair. It normally takes from eight to twenty-four hours for the body to go into "cleanse" mode. Cleanse mode happens when the liver does not have to worry about digestion and realizes it is free to start cleaning things it had previously backlogged. The liver and the body literally work their way through everything that has been stored since your birth. During a fast, particularly your first fast, you will literally relive every illness and injury you have ever had that the liver did not have time to fully repair. During my first eleven-day juice fast, on various days I experienced everything from a fever and chills, to swollen lymph nodes, to knee and shoulder pain from old volleyball injuries. This may sound kind of nasty, but the individual pains do not last long, a few hours at most, and for the vast majority of my eleven-day fast, I felt great and had more energy than I ever had.

Some people lose a lot of weight while fasting; others do not, but most people lose *sizes*. The body gets rid of all the toxins that make us look "puffy." I dropped to a size 4 from a size 8 and only lost one pound during my eleven-day fast. After an initial fast, I recommend fasting as much as you can over the next several years. Some people do this by fasting one day per week or doing one three-day fast per month. Always listen to your body. If you feel like fasting, do it; this happens to most of us naturally in the summertime. If you are hungry—eat and don't force anything after the initial fast—your body is telling you what it needs.

5 Tips for a Successful Juice Fast
1. Drink 8–16 eight-ounce glasses of freshly pressed juices, vegetable broths, and herbal teas. Nothing can have added sugar of any kind, and all chemicals are to be avoided. For best results, use fresh juices, but pasteurized juices will suffice if necessary (once again, never with sugar added).
2. Avoid tomato, orange, and grapefruit juices. Although all of these juices have a positive alkalizing effect on the body's cells, each is very acidic, which encourages the stomach to produce stomach acid—stomach acid makes us feel hungry. We want to avoid the release of stomach acid and the feeling of hunger on a fast whenever possible!
3. Avoid moderate and strenuous exercise. This is to prevent hunger pains and conserve your energy for healing and detoxifying the body. Experienced fasters can sometimes handle moderate exercise, but it is not recommended for beginners.

4. Drink vegetable juices and herbal teas in the morning (before 2:00 p.m.). Then if you must have fruit juices, have them sparingly after 2:00 p.m. This avoids spiking your blood sugar early in the day when the body is in its most acidic state. The three exceptions to this are cranberry juice (plain with no sugar added; this will be incredibly sour), lemon, and lime juice. These three can be sipped at any time; cranberry is especially good first thing in the morning if you have any kidney problems. (If you have any liver problems or candida/parasites, you most likely will have weak kidneys, because the kidneys have been filtering everything the stressed liver could not process.)

5. Drink warm vegetable broths or bone broths if you get hungry or want something warm. (It is great to warm the body on a fast because your body temperature will naturally drop, and warm liquids can by-pass hunger pains.) Boil cubed potatoes or turnips, carrots, celery, onions, and garlic for at least twenty minutes—drink just the broth; you can add some sea salt if you would like. Organic sugar-free broths can also be purchased from organic grocers.

Some fasting books recommend eating fresh watermelon or fresh applesauce (puree a fresh apple) when you feel you *must* eat. I do not recommend this; anytime you chew or have something sit in the mouth for extended periods of time, the stomach is activated, and this always makes me hungrier, and I feel worse. (Chewing gum has the same effect and must be avoided!) If you are extremely hungry or are detoxing too quickly, you can do the apple puree but water it down enough so you can *drink* it. The apple fiber gives the body something to bind to the toxins, which reduces the detox symptoms and makes you feel full.

* * *

Juice experts debate about whether a juice fast or a puree fast is better. A puree fast keeps the fiber with the juice. I think both are good, and it depends on the person, but the juice fast will always be more intense and encourage a faster detox; this is why many people avoid the juice fast and do purees instead. The fiber slows the detoxification process down and minimizes the symptoms. I accomplish the same physical results on a three-day juice fast that would take me six or seven days if I was using fruit and vegetable purees. My personal preference is to just get it all done and out of my system as quickly as possible—I would rather risk being uncomfortable for a few days instead of mildly uncomfortable for a week, but we are all different; my husband prefers purees for a week over juice-fasting for several days.

When you enter a fasting state, you are shifting your energy inward and giving your body time to heal itself. Stay warm; it is much easier to fast in the spring and summer. Be sure to put aside as much time to yourself as possible during each day you fast. A fast induces a sort of illness state, and the body wants to be left alone to withdraw and heal. The more time you can allocate to yourself and letting go of the emotions that surface, the more effective the fast will be. I have fasted at home alone, and I have fasted while at work. The important thing is to keep your mind busy and off of food. Very light exercise is good to keep the energy flowing and the pathways of detox open and moving; walking, light yoga and stretching, tai chi, or qigong work well.

If we were naturally in tune with everything in our bodies like Mother Nature intended, we would instinctively know when to fast, and we would retreat. In today's fast-paced society, it is more difficult to listen to our inner voice when the outside world is frantic. Native Americans went on vision quests, fasting until the answer they sought appeared to them; Buddhist monks typically eat two meals a day before noon and nothing after lunch; and religiously decreed fasts attempted to recreate the experience of turning within. During the Islamic holy month of Ramadan, no food or liquid is consumed during daylight. Fasting has varied through time in Christianity[1]—sometimes two weekdays were devoted to fasting, and often major fasts aligned with the seasonal changes four times a year.

Modern society includes many toxins our ancestors never experienced: pollution, food and water laden with chemicals (fluoride and chlorine), vaccinations, physical trauma and surgeries; our liver has to handle all of this in addition to the "normal" stresses of life. We control our environment to the extent we can: the food we eat, the water we drink, the technological waves in our homes—and then we can fast for extra support.

* * *

Supplements and Tips to Relieve Detox Symptoms

1. Coffee Enemas. See chapter on "The 'E' Word—Enemas." This is absolutely the quickest, most efficient way to eliminate detox headaches and pains. Do as little as one a day or as many as one per hour.
2. NAC (N-Acetyl-Cysteine) is great for overall toxin relief; it helps the liver deal with the pollutants more effectively. It is actually a precursor amino acid for the powerful antioxidant glutathione. NAC is great for detox headaches and body pains. Even the medical community is beginning to admit the benefits of this powerful source of liver support. The body needs NAC to make glutathione, which is actually what is neutralizing the toxins in the body. Glutathione supplements are sold; however, the cheap ones are unstable and not absorbed well by the body. There are some brands that are absorbable and stable; however, they are much more expensive than NAC.
3. Milk thistle is an herb that can help protect the liver and minimize detox symptoms.
4. Powdered vitamin C is wonderful for all detox symptoms because vitamin C neutralizes several major toxins in the body that will be eliminated during the fast—a food source (like acerola cherry powder) is always best!
5. MSM (methylsulfonylmethane) is great for anything that feels like allergies (runny nose, congestion, hives) and also joint pains to some extent. MSM is a natural source of sulfur. (MSM should be from an organic food source and not the petroleum industry.)
6. Green tea can be good for headaches and detox from heavy metal chelation but use sparingly on a fast because of the caffeine.
7. Chlorella and spirulina are blue-green algae that are packed with vitamins, minerals, and amino acids. Both are excellent toxin-neutralizers and provide bioavailable protein while fasting.

8. Fiber mixed with bentonite clay. Apple pectin tablets scrub the colon, and it, or other fiber sources, can be combined with bentonite clay or hydrated bentonite clay to absorb toxins out of the small/large intestine and help minimize detox symptoms. This is a great way to reduce painful symptoms and rid the body of toxins. Note: anything consumed within ninety minutes of the bentonite clay will be absorbed by it, so be sure to save its absorption powers for your toxic colon and not any healthy foods or juices along the way.

Avoid all over-the-counter or pharmaceutical drugs (this means no Tylenol or Advil). All synthetic drugs put extreme stress on the liver and other detoxification organs.

Drinking herbal teas, infusions, or tinctures during a fast can help support the liver by providing targeted nutrients to cleanse the blood, the colon, or the immune system. Infusions are strong teas where the plant material is soaked overnight or for at least eight hours after boiling it. Please visit www.equilibriumdiet.com for the fasting benefits of various herbs.

Please note that some nutritionists and scientists criticize fasting because of the strain it puts on the adrenal glands. This criticism usually only applies to a strict water or herbal tea fast where the person is not taking in calories. With a juice fast, drinking eight to twelve glasses of fresh juices a day, the adrenals are not nearly as stressed. For the vast majority of people, any adrenal stress is less than what they experience while on the standard American diet, laden with caffeine, processed food, wheat, and sugar—all four place extreme burdens on the adrenal glands. This group of people could fast and see quick and dramatic benefits from the fast within days. If you feel you simply cannot fast, look into kitchari—kitchari is an Ayurvedic recipe with rice and mung beans that can be used instead of a water or juice fast to minimize the body's digestive burden.

CHAPTER 22

Colon, Kidney, Parasite, Heavy Metal Cleanses, and the Liver Flush

The best *colon cleanses* are usually a blend of herbs and plant enzymes and some form of fiber. These can be purchased premixed in tablet form, or you can buy the individual herbs and mix them. I recommend the former, because it tends to be easier and cheaper unless the individual has a severe reaction to a particular herb used. Herbal *kidney cleanses* are also available premixed and usually taken as a tea. Most people will not have a reaction to a mixture of herbs even if they are intolerant to one particular herb by itself. The best way to ensure an herbal formula is good for you is with vibrational or energetic testing. If an individual is ever weak for a substance, it should not be consumed.

* * *

Parasite Cleanses

With a juice fast that is low in fruit juices (natural sugars), any parasites and critters will naturally get killed off if you fast for long enough. If you want additional ammunition and/or think you may have some serious critters like liver flukes (very common from eating raw fish), you may want to embark on a parasite cleanse. Most parasite cleanses are herb based and aim to create a hostile environment for the resilient, toxin-eating critters. In general, once the toxins and sugar that provide the food to the parasites are eliminated, the parasites die off naturally. Herbal formulas help hasten the process.

The major parasite killers here are black walnut and wormwood. Clove, garlic, grapefruit seed extract, pau d'arco, and pumpkin seeds are also good. However, if you are allergic to walnuts, like me, you are usually out of luck when it comes to finding a pre-manufactured formula, because black walnut is almost always the number-one ingredient; it is *that* effective. There are a few blends without it; however, they can be tough to find, so I usually end up putting together my own cleanse using wormwood, clove, garlic, pumpkin seed, pau d'arco, and an enzyme blend to cut through all of the dead stuff. The enzymes help the body rip apart and digest all those dead critters—gross, I know, but better out than in!

* * *

Heavy Metal Cleanse

Heavy metals are everywhere and do serious damage. In our polluted environment, we all have heavy metals to some extent. Symptoms of heavy metal toxicity include fatigue, chronic diseases, allergies, dark circles under the eyes, skin rashes, memory and thought problems, and in extreme cases—insanity. Chelating (removing) heavy metals from the body is a process that pays off immediately and in the long run. The key is to begin chelating slowly and at low doses so you don't suffer the pains of feeling the metals in your system, and so that the metals don't get reabsorbed during the process. Different heavy metals are chelated best with different agents, but the cilantro cleanse is cheap, easy, and will pull out a lot of mercury and other heavy metals. To perform this cleanse, you need three supplements: cilantro, chlorella, and apple pectin.

I would recommend completing the seven-day (or longer) juice fast, then beginning the Equilibrium Diet along with a parasite cleanse (days 1–29), and then a heavy metal detox (days 30–51). For a person with a clean diet and colon, I would actually recommend the reverse order (heavy metal cleanse followed by the parasite cleanse). Regardless of the order, the key to the heavy metal cleanse is that the colon has to be moving waste efficiently so that the chelated metals are not sitting around for days.

When heavy metals are present, the body and liver actually want to keep parasites (particularly candida) around, because the critters buffer the heavy metals from severely damaging the body—the body chooses to live with the waste created from the candida instead of suffering the full extent of exposure to heavy metals. The body chooses the lesser of two evils—candida side effects: like a feeling of drunkenness, white-coated tongue, imprecise thinking, prostatitis, skin problems, sinus pain and congestion, and constipation. When heavy metals are present, having candida is actually an equilibrium state for the body. One can only improve and get rid of candida once the root of the condition is gone—heavy metals is one of them. The heavy metal detox is really easy. You just need to eat well (follow the Equilibrium Diet) and have four supplements on hand. You will take the following for six days and then take two days off. Repeat the six-on, two-off cycle for thirty-two days (four cycles). Always start with small amounts of cilantro and generous portions of chlorella and pectin. This ensures that all of the metals are properly neutralized and bound for removal.

1. **Cilantro** (fresh or as a tincture) chelates heavy metals. It literally pulls them out of the brain, the joints, and the rest of the body. Eat one handful two times per day or take the recommended dosage on the tincture bottle two times per day (before breakfast and dinner).

2. **Chlorella** are blue-green sea algae that neutralize the heavy metals that the cilantro pulls out. The heavy metals will continue to circulate and eventually relocate unless the toxins are neutralized. Green tea can also do this, but chlorella is the best. I will usually drink green tea along with the chlorella for extra support. Take six to eight tablets (or a serving size), twice a day thirty minutes before taking the cilantro. This ensures the chlorella is in the correct place in the small intestine to neutralize the metals when the liver begins dumping them.

3. **Apple pectin** provides the fiber needed for the body to take the neutralized heavy metal, bind it, and eliminate it through the colon. Take one to two tablets twice a day a few minutes before taking the chlorella. For example, if you wake up at 6:00 a.m. and take six chlorella tablets, ten minutes later take two pectin tablets. Twenty minutes after the pectin, take five to ten drops of cilantro in water. Do this again before dinner or at bedtime.

The important aspect of the heavy metal detox is to take the chlorella slightly before the cilantro because the chlorella needs to move into the small intestine before the cilantro starts chelating. I recommend waiting about twenty to thirty minutes; you'll know if you have waited too long (or need more chlorella), because you will start to get a headache and feel like your head is "swimming in toxins."(And it will be without that chlorella!) If you accidentally take too much cilantro or begin chelating too quickly, there are several back-up remedies, but they are just that—back-ups. Each attempts to minimize the damage in the midst of a painful detox. Chelating too quickly can cause severe headaches, lymph node pain, chest pains, joint pains, blurry vision, eye pain, body aches, nausea, and moodiness. If you begin to feel any of these symptoms, implement a few of the following remedies.

- Take more chlorella.
- Take hydrated bentonite clay from a reputable source (some bentonite contains aluminum, so buy the best quality possible).
- Take milk thistle or MSM.
- Take N-Acetyl-Cysteine, L-Lysine, and/or L-methionine.
- Drink lots of green tea.
- Take a hot bath with Epsom salts, or vitamin C, or green tea. Vitamin C tablets for the bath can be purchased online or at most stores as "de-chlorinating" agents. Each of these will help draw out toxins and help the body to neutralize the toxins. Make sure to soap and rinse off with fresh water when you get out of the bath to neutralize anything on the skin.

Notes on chelation: In professional chelation therapies, all metals (good and bad) are removed. This is not the case with cilantro chelation, so mineral supplementation is not required.

Remember, any chemical you put on your skin will be absorbed and pass through to your liver for detoxification. Candida can also overrun the body when the body's environment is too high in toxic substances. Drink only clean water, and drink enough of it. Minimize or eliminate exposure to bleach, chemicals, and pesticides, which includes fragrances, lotions, and perfumes—anything you put on your skin or a baby's skin should be a 100 percent food-grade oil. (All petroleum-based products do *not* fall in this category, including

Vaseline, petroleum jelly, most lotions, sunscreens, shampoos, conditioners, soaps, and diaper creams.) See www.equilibriumdiet.com for a list of all-natural substitute products.

* * *

Liver Flushes

Liver flushes drastically reduce the toxic load your liver is carrying around and increase the liver's effectiveness. Liver flushes are wonderful for chronic illnesses, allergies, gallbladder problems, hormonal imbalances, high cholesterol, and high blood pressure. The liver controls so much that a liver flush is a great, relatively easy way to quickly improve your health with minimal costs. There are entire books on the history and science behind liver flushes; I have provided a general overview of this time-tested remedy here.[1]

All gallstones begin in the liver as liver stones and then move down the bile duct and get lodged in the gallbladder where they may calcify into hard stones. A liver flush naturally sucks out some of the gallstones and liver stones by encouraging the body to drop the stones into the small intestine to then be eliminated through the stool. I believe that ad-hoc liver flushes were included in most major religions. (Though Islam, Judaism, and Buddhism do not refer to the events as liver flushes, but fasting followed by high-fat meals elicits the same bodily response—I learned this experientially!) There are many variations on the liver flush, but here are the basics for a pain-free experience. Remember, the liver flush should not be attempted until one has eaten a diet free from sugar, preservatives, and refined foods for at least thirty days.

1. Drink apple juice or malic acid for six days (32 ounces per day between meals).
2. During the six days of apple juice, be sure to follow the Equilibrium Diet, which avoids caffeine, meat at night, sugar, refined products, and processed food.
3. On the sixth day, you will drink all of your apple juice between breakfast and lunch (all 32 ounces), and you should not eat or drink anything but water after 2:00 p.m.

4.	At 6:00 p.m. on the sixth day, drink Epsom salt water (3/4 cup water with 1 tablespoon Epsom salt, also called magnesium sulfate).
5.	At 8:00 p.m., drink another 3/4 cup of Epsom salt water.
6.	At 10:00 p.m., perform the actual flush. Mix 3/4 cup of fresh squeezed grapefruit juice with 1/2 cup of extra virgin olive oil. Pour in a glass jar and shake vigorously. Chug immediately and lie down in bed on your back; focus on your liver for 20 minutes and then go to sleep.
7.	At 6:00 a.m. and 8:00 a.m. the next morning, drink additional rounds of 3/4 cup water and 1 tablespoon Epsom salts.
8.	At 9:00 a.m., you may start eating/drinking normally but lightly. Your body has just undergone big changes, so take it easy on your liver for the next few days!

The flush works by using the malic acid in apple juice to soften the stones; this makes the stones easier to pass and loosens them from the liver tissues. The apple juice should never include added sugar. If you are sensitive to the natural fruit sugar, you can replace all, or part, of the thirty-two ounces a day with raw apple cider vinegar (two tablespoons = one glass or eight ounces of apple juice), some cranberry juice, or malic acid powder in water. I have always seen the best results using just apple juice (and sometimes a little apple cider vinegar added to the apple juice).

The magnesium sulfate softens the bile ducts so the stones can pass through pain-free. You may feel some gurgling or movement as the stones trickle down, but you will not feel the pain of a "gallbladder attack" when drinking the Epsom salt water. It is also a mild laxative and will help wash all of the stones out of your colon the next day (and clean it out the night before so the stones won't get stuck)!

The olive oil and citrus carry a strong negative charge, and the stones are positively charged. A sort of magnetic attraction occurs, and the stones rush out to meet the negatively charged oil mixture. I have done several accidental liver flushes using homemade coconut oil fudge; however, I never get many stones using this "accidental" method—probably because I didn't have the six days of malic acid to soften the stones, and the fudge isn't amplified by any citrus. Some nausea is common during your first liver flush because so many stones are flushed that they back up into the stomach cavity (this usually occurs in the middle of the night and will pass eventually). Even with the risk of nausea, the results of the liver flush are well worth the cost, offering immediate increases in energy, flexibility, and mental sharpness. The key to the liver flush is to keep doing them every four to six weeks until you do not pass any stones. For most people, this may take six to twelve flushes. I had to flush probably ten times before I didn't see any stones, and I've passed thousands of liver stones ranging in size from a pinhead to almost golf-ball sized.

You want to be sure to get all of the stones out; you do not want them stuck in the intestines from eating constipating foods. This is why I list the liver flush as the last cleanse; the bowels should be accustomed to quality food and moving regularly by the time you do a liver flush. To prevent stones from getting stuck, follow the liver flush directions precisely; when you have completed the flush, you can do several coffee enemas to encourage stone elimination. You could have a colonic session (colon hydrotherapy) or use a colenema board (essentially, an at-home colonic). Lastly, you can take a specific magnesium powder known to oxygenate and clear the colon (Coloson). I use the Coloson and coffee enemas, and I have never had any problems. I suggest reading *The Amazing Liver and Gallbladder Flush* by Andres Moritz for all the details.

There are several Internet sites that try to discredit the liver flush. In most cases, the authors are criticizing something they clearly have not tried. One criticism is that the olive oil is just coagulating in the intestines, and that is what people are defecating and seeing. I personally kept doing flushes until no more stones came out; if coagulation was the only action happening, everyone should see stones with every flush—this is not the case. I also did mini-liver flushes in the middle of gallbladder attacks with instant relief. This may not be for everyone, but it has worked extremely well for me and the people I have worked with!

CHAPTER 23

Detox Support

The path to wellness is not always easy. Just finding a group of people who eat healthily may provide the backbone you need to keep pushing along. Please consider joining the Equilibrium Diet's Facebook page for a *support group online* where you can find a community of people experiencing similar things; you can also post any question to me or the group. My husband and I were on our own; we were each other's backbone. If we could not find research on a topic on the Internet, we did not have any other human source to fall back on. There were times where we felt completely alone and ostracized from society. Most of our family, friends, and colleagues initially mocked our "unconventional" approach to nutrition. Often we felt like we could not talk to anyone around us about what we were going through.

We learned that nutrition and diet should be classed right up there with politics and religion as conversational topics that fire people up. People get very defensive about their own lifestyle choices when confronted with new ways of looking at the world. When you present a theory and supporting evidence for having control over your own health and your own life, some people find that empowering, but others find it terrifying. For those on this path, trust yourself and your process.

The need for an *emotional support group* will become increasingly apparent during your journey. You are beginning a new way of life, a new way of thinking about yourself, and this involves the death of the old you and your old patterns and thoughts. Detoxing is a physical, emotional, and mental journey—the emotions will come. As you detox, every organ in your body will release the toxins it has been holding for years. And when an organ is detoxing, you will feel the symptoms of that organ. Embrace the change and know that you are on the right path. It is a phase, and it will pass—just keep plugging along.

The scariest phase of our journey was when our thyroids detoxed—we were anxious and paranoid that we were never going to get better. There were times I thought I had crazy, unheard-of illnesses. These are all emotional issues from candida die-off and detox. The brain is starting to function normally again as all the candida and other critters die off, and the body begins rebuilding the glandular system.

If you stick to the layout in this book, which is fairly aggressive, the thyroid detox will probably last from six to eight weeks. At this stage, I highly recommend reading Debbie Ford's *The Dark Side of the Light Chasers* and any sort of "shadow" workbook. Shadow work during this introspective phase allows you to release more of the mental and emotional toxicity and move through the detox more quickly. A large part of this is listening to your body. It will say, "Look at all of this baggage and clutter you have accumulated and not taken the time to sort through. You have bags from your mom, your dad, your grandma, and your grade-school teachers. You have carried all of this mess around with you for years. There is nothing to learn; just let it go."

* * *

Alternative medicine offers many modalities that can reduce and even eliminate most detox symptoms. Acupuncture, hands-on or "touch" kinesiology, massage, Network Chiropractics, breath work, and TRE are all helpful tools to keep the body in alignment as your body detoxifies. *Acupuncture* uses hair-fine needles to stimulate the energy passageways in and around the body. It is wonderful to break up congestion and stagnation anywhere in the body. *Kinesiology* is a hybrid of reiki and massage where the body is rubbed and energy centers "activated" to help release physical and emotional blockages. Some *chiropractors* are more like kinesiologists and will push and massage the muscles to get them to relax and release the bones so that they may move back into proper alignment. Other chiropractors crack the bones back into place without working on the muscles first. Network chiropractors, taught by Donny Epstein, do not crack or forcefully touch the body at all.

Breath work focuses on the spiritual connection between the breath and the body. It theorizes that when we hold our breath out of fear or trauma, the event is then stored in our tissues. Breath work or "rebirthing" aims to heal old patterns or trauma by breathing through them. Observing a breath work session, you can often see the body unconsciously realign itself with cracks as loud as those performed by a chiropractor as old events are released. The great thing about breath work is you can actually do it yourself once you have attended a few sessions; this cannot be said for many other methods. I recommend reading *The Presence Process* by Michael Brown for a good introduction into using breath work yourself at home. There are also many breath work practitioners and groups in most areas in the United States and Europe.

TRE (trauma release exercises) is a free stress-release program you can do at home anytime. Simply look up TRE on YouTube to see examples and how-to videos. Essentially, TRE teaches people to activate their psoas muscle, which shakes and twitches out the cortisol stored in the body. This is one of my favorite modalities, because it is free, you can do it alone, and it releases the unconscious trauma without us having to experience or see it at all. I have done this watching TV and with my kids screaming to trigger my subconscious to release stored tension pertaining to TV and screaming children!

Each of these different methods of aligning the body appeals to different people. It does not matter which you prefer; you simply want the passages of waste removal to be clear and flowing when you begin releasing years of built-up gunk. If your detox symptoms are intense, vibrational practitioners can help (I have had success with homeopathy, Total Body Analysis, Holographic Health, and NAET). Sometimes that left brain and the ego stir up a "storm of resistance" to get you to give up or go back to your old ways. This is the process of remembering and trusting yourself. When a thought "pops" into your head, trust that the information is exactly what you need at that time to answer your question. If you don't happen to have an acupuncturist or kinesiologist, or other alternative healer nearby, any of the exercise programs in the next section are excellent to help the energy pathways clear and remain clear during physical, mental, and emotional detox. Most of the exercise programs can be done with a DVD in your own home.

* * *

Exercise

I find that *movement* is more important than exercise, and so most of these modalities are very low impact. Qigong, tai chi, yoga, and dance are great exercises to keep the body's energy flowing and the waste-removal passages open. Really, any exercise program that gets the energies moving will suffice. Qigong and tai chi are Asian programs that focus on the energies around and inside the body. Yoga and dance also get the blood and energy pumping. Try a few different programs and see which one speaks to you.

If you have worked out for extended periods of time in your life, do not be surprised if you have no desire to do anything, or anything high impact for a long time. Often such extensive periods of exercise tip the body out of balance, and only time and "no exercise" can eventually pull the body back into equilibrium. You may literally recover from an "excess of exercise." As always, listen to your body—to the voice deep inside of you that says, "I've had too much of this—I need to give it a rest for a while so I can reach a new, higher state of equilibrium."

* * *

Improvement and the Healing Crisis

I found that in terms of the order of improvement, the "oldest problems" are the last to go because they are most ingrained in the body, and the "newest problems" are the first to resolve. Most holistic medical models draw the same conclusion. In general, weight and blood sugar are the first to stabilize. Because the stable blood then feeds the rest of the body, the rest of the body slowly follows suit. The energy level in the body varies from stage to stage and seems to increase, or decrease, depending on what organ is detoxing and how depleted the adrenal glands are. The high blood flow areas seem to be the first to return to balance: the brain, the heart, and the major internal organs. These are followed by the digestive system and pancreas. The last areas to return to balance seem to be the low blood flow areas. These are the areas your body could maybe do without when it is desperate for nutrients and conservation. Your body is going to protect your brain and heart at all costs, but low blood flow areas like the ovaries, prostate, appendix, gallbladder, and spleen are typically the first organs to display problems and the last to make a full recovery. They all have vital functions, but when your body is trying to survive, it doesn't worry about reproduction or sex drive. Along the blood-flow line, the prostate doesn't get much; it gets the leftovers. Same with the appendix, gallbladder, and spleen; all help detoxify the body, but they are second lines of defense. The skin and the blood are the first line of defense; the liver is the primary cleanser, with backup from the spleen, kidneys, and gallbladder.

And remember that the body works in leaps and bounds, not gradually. This means that cheating on your diet can be detrimental at certain stages. Every second, your cells are battling the foreigners. When they are losing, you have symptoms, but then one day they become strong enough with the good nutrients you've been feeding them, and they have just enough strength to overtake the critters and regain control of your body. You will feel this when all of a sudden your left ear drains, or you wake up after six hours of sleep feeling refreshed and exuberant! The immune system is usually the first to become depleted and will be the last to heal completely. The thymus, thyroid, spleen, and sinuses seem to regenerate in the final stages of healing. This could take two to four years after your initial change. Granted you will feel much, much better and will probably feel 100 percent healthy even before these areas are totally healed. We live in a relative world, and you will know how much better you feel compared to where you were when you began—and even just a few months earlier.

In cases of illness—bacterial, viral, candida, parasitic—it is important to realize that the "critters" seriously impair cell nourishment. After years of depletion, cells may need some TLC even after the critters are gone. The digestive track will be damaged; good bacteria, iron, and B-12 may be seriously low, making supplementation helpful. Once again, these are all related to the immune system, which would have been the first to be compromised when the body invited the critters to the buffet of waste.

Remember, most of us have years—lifetimes—of stored toxicity in our bodies. Initially, switching to a clean diet can create a "healing crisis" when old symptoms make their way out of the body. Do not suppress the symptoms of a healing crisis with pharmaceuticals. We want those energy patterns out! Initially, the healing crisis will be largely physical; you may have brain fog, muscle aches, and skin eruptions—all signs of healing. (Remember, acupuncture and vibrational practices like homeopathy, Total Body Analysis, and Holographic Health can eliminate most cleansing reactions.) As you continue to eat healthier, suppressed emotions may begin to surface; acknowledge them and let them go. Then you will feel better than you have felt in your entire life. We are all, all things; we contain all of the whole. So in order to return to the whole, we must accept all that we are: joyful, beautiful, successful, angry, depressed, vengeful, suicidal, plus every other characteristic (both positive and negative). All repressed emotions will come through as you attain higher and higher levels of health. This is your body releasing years of DNA trauma—it's normal. Six years after beginning this dietary change, I still have emotions and thought forms coming through to be released. Such is the path of loving *all* of ourselves.

CHAPTER 24

Create Your Own Ninety-Day Program

I know you may be feeling a bit overwhelmed by the amount of sheer information we have covered. I want to reiterate that Lance and I changed gradually and that you can change as quickly or as slowly as you desire. Do only what you feel comfortable with—*maybe* push your own boundaries a little bit. I have listed every cleanse we ever did and compiled the entire diet so you know the entire path we took. That does not mean you have to make all the changes overnight. Granted, the more you do, the more quickly you and your world will get healthier. I have included a timeline below that includes all of our major dietary changes and spiritual events. I hope this will help you to estimate where you are on your own journey and what your next steps could be. As you can see, we didn't eliminate wheat until almost eight months into the diet; we didn't eliminate dairy entirely until over eighteen months on the diet.

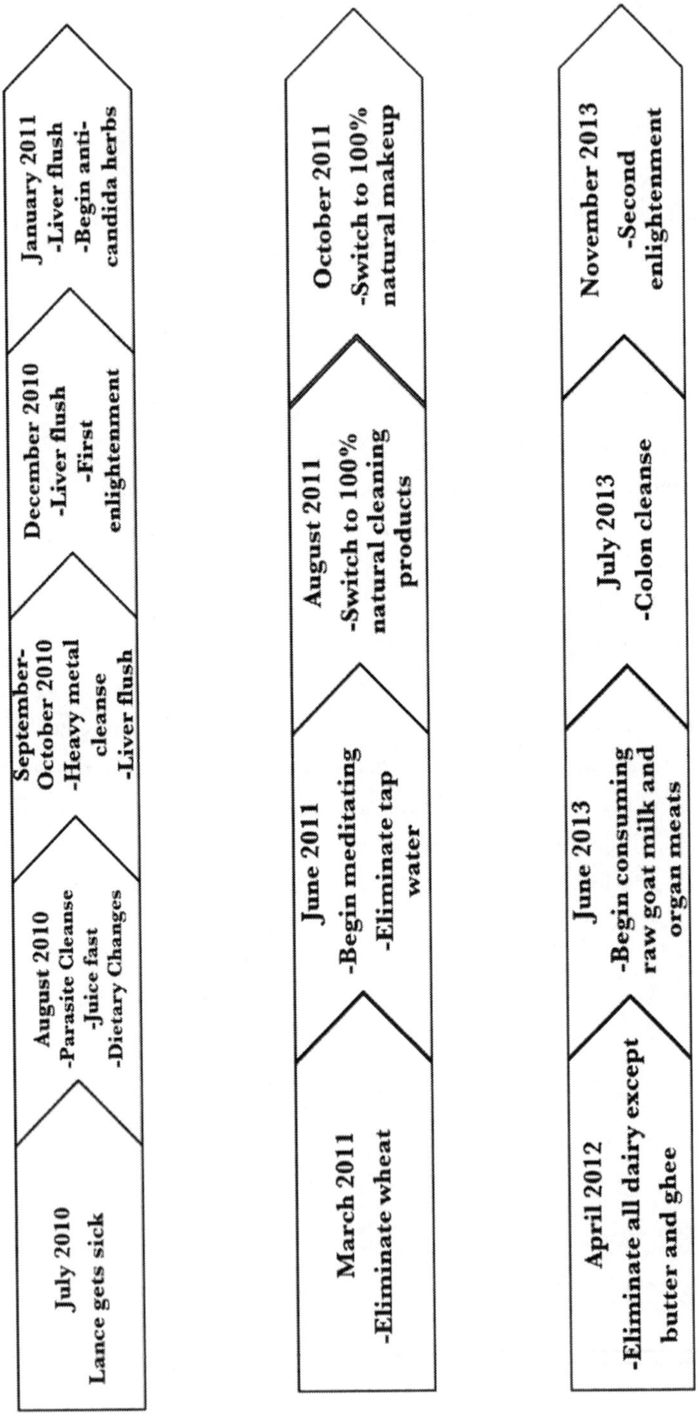
July 2010
Lance gets sick
August 2010
-Parasite Cleanse
-Juice fast
-Dietary Changes
September-October 2010
-Heavy metal cleanse
-Liver flush
December 2010
-Liver flush
-First enlightenment
January 2011
-Liver flush
-Begin anti-candida herbs
March 2011
-Eliminate wheat
June 2011
-Begin meditating
-Eliminate tap water
August 2011
-Switch to 100% natural cleaning products
October 2011
-Switch to 100% natural makeup
April 2012
-Eliminate all dairy except butter and ghee
June 2013
-Begin consuming raw goat milk and organ meats
July 2013
-Colon cleanse
November 2013
-Second enlightenment

For those who would like to take the challenge and begin their own path to enlightenment, health, and happiness, I have created a step-by-step program to guide you through each phase. In each phase, participants will be asked to choose an activity or two from the included list to aid in the detox process. This is the process of *remembering*; it is a path that unwinds, reminding us that we are all conscious beings here to live out a purpose on the earth. In general, participants completing all ninety days and solidifying their new habits will experience the following during the months of the program and beyond:

After 30 days	Newfound energy, more restful sleep. Stable blood sugar and no sugar cravings. Lose one to two clothing sizes unless already thin.
After 60 days	Moods stabilize, tempers cool down, overall a happier disposition. Continue to lose clothing sizes as diet continues.
After 90 days	Increased body awareness. Your body and mind may begin to open to new sensations, and the sixth sense may intensify; this can be more acute for women and most acute for pregnant women. Continue to lose clothing sizes as diet continues.
After 4 months	Begin to feel the energy world and vibrations. The sensations will come from you and other people; it becomes increasingly important to meditate and take time to sift through which emotions and thoughts are yours and which are not. This begins the process of trusting yourself and what you are experiencing. Begin the process of releasing (through shadow work) the old gunk. Continue to lose clothing sizes as diet continues.
After 6 months	Enlightenment or a spiritual experience. (This may take longer, but it *will* happen.) The moment of awakening. Increased immunity and more energy—all health ailments begin to fade away.

Days 1–10 Juice Fast

Before 2:00 p.m., consume at least thirty-two ounces of vegetable juices and broths, preferably raw and unpasteurized.

After 2:00 p.m., consume at least thirty-two ounces of all-natural vegetable and fruit juices. Drinking the fruit juices only in the afternoon helps stabilize blood sugar and prevents hunger pains.

Use coffee enemas as needed. (The more the merrier while fasting!)

Choose 1–2 of the following activities each day for all 90 days
1. **The Brain Drain**. Write three unedited, unfiltered pages by hand of anything that pops in your head. Do not stop writing and start "thinking" until you have reached the end of the third page. This is a technique from one of my favorite books, *The Artist's Way* by Julia Cameron.
2. Light yoga or stretching
3. Qigong or tai chi
4. Low-intensity nature walk
5. Ten minutes of silent meditation
6. **Shadow work**. There are many versions available. Find the one that most speaks to you. I recommend reading and working through Debbie Ford's book, *The Dark Side of the Light Chasers*, which can be followed by Lao Tzu's *Tao Te Ching*.
To speed up your process, you may also want to choose one of the following activities: body work—massage therapy, acupuncture, breath work, or TRE.

Days 11–12 **Break the fast with warming broths, steamed rice and veggies, and fresh fruit.** Or if it is summertime, raw vegetables can be consumed instead.

Days 13–34 **Heavy metal cleanse or optional parasite cleanse.** In order to excrete the heavy metals, the colon must be moving and eliminating wastes at least twice a day. A ten-day juice fast should be enough to rejuvenate the digestive and elimination systems for most people. If your bowels are not moving at least two times per day once you break your fast, then begin an herbal parasite cleanse instead of the heavy metal cleanse. *Coffee enemas as needed.*

Days 13–34 **The heavy metal cleanse should be performed for six days on, two days off. The twenty-two-day cleanse will provide three cycles of cleansing for six days.**

Twice a day (morning and evening), take six chlorella tablets and one apple pectin tablet twenty minutes before taking five drops of cilantro extract in water. Drink lots of water. Follow the Equilibrium Diet.

Days 35–40 **Liver Flush**

Eat according to the Equilibrium Diet and follow all liver flush instructions using coffee enemas as needed (one per day unless detox symptoms arise).

Days 40–46 **The Equilibrium Diet and Building Your Body's Vitamin and Mineral Inventories**

Seven-day break from cleanses. Optional coffee enemas.

Days 47–71 **Kidney Cleanse (twenty-five days)**

Days 72–78 **The Equilibrium Diet and Building Your Body's Vitamin and Mineral Inventories**

Seven-day break from cleanses. Optional coffee enemas.

Days 79–81 **Juice Fast (three days)**

Days 82–87 **Liver Flush (or) Heavy Metal Cleanse**

Days 88–90+ **Building with the Equilibrium Diet**

Congratulations! You have completed a blueprint to rediscovering yourself and locked in the new pattern. Keep it up and share your out-of-this-world experiences at https://www.facebook.com/equilibriumdiet!

CHAPTER 25

Questions and Answer

I have provided brief answers to the most commonly asked questions regarding the Equilibrium Diet and my journey. Questions pertaining to the Equilibrium Diet are listed first and are followed by the more general questions asked about my journey in part 1.

I have children. Can they follow the Equilibrium Diet and do the cleansing program with me?

Eating according to the Equilibrium Diet is efficient for *everyone*, regardless of age. Children, regardless of age, can detox and usually do so more gracefully than adults. Initially, children and teens may complain or even refuse to eat the new healthy foods; however, they experience critter die-off just like adults do and all of the cravings that go with it. I know of several families where the children simply refused to eat anything during the initial weeks following the dietary changes. The kids are fasting just like we do, though perhaps unintentionally. One two-year-old refused to eat anything for almost three full *weeks* and demanded McDonald's and sugary cereals. The parents held firm, and today, the whole family is sugar-free, dairy-free, and gluten-free. It is important to remember that kids are just like adults; eating low-quality food just to eat *something* and "have food in your belly" is actually worse for the body than eating *nothing*. I understand the protective urge of parents to "just get the kids to eat," but just relax and know that once your children's bodies are ready for high-quality food, they will eat it. Before that, let the cleansing cycle run its course and don't give into your, or your children's, demands for sugary, life-sucking foods. Remember, the nutritional return the body yields on each meal or snack must be positive for the vast majority of meals to eradicate nutritional bankruptcy. Meals containing sugar, processed food, fast food, and pasteurized dairy will not meet the standard of excellence needed to support nutritional solvency.

In regards to the lifestyle cleanses, do what you are comfortable with for your kids. Many companies now make cleanses specifically for children, or find a local vibrational practitioner who can assist you and your children with the detox. Some children don't need much physical support (like herbs), because they've had less time to damage their bodies. Especially for young children, the vibrational supplements like homeopaths and flower essences may be all they need to minimize detox symptoms and begin enjoying wellness. Infants, children, and teens on the Equilibrium Diet report sleeping better, fewer illnesses, fewer emotional outbursts, increased concentration, better athletic performance, and clearer skin. All age appropriate, of course!

I began the ninety-day program, and the temptation was too much for my favorite sweet treat, and I ate it. What should I do?

First, try to take it easy on yourself. The important thing to ask yourself in this moment is, "Why do I desire this sugary food?" This will always be for one of two reasons: 1) low protein or 2) a painful emotion is about to surface, and you are subconsciously attempting to block it. Both may feel like cravings, so it can take time to distinguish which we are actually experiencing, but the first will go away with a high-protein snack. When we haven't had enough protein early in the day, the body sends the signal that it needs energy in the form of glucose—a sugar craving. In this case, try to eat an extra ten grams of protein the next morning. (In the meantime, try drinking a tall glass of raw goat's milk—the body can use this protein at virtually no cost.) A high-protein snack will *not* eliminate the craving if an emotion is surfacing. In this case, quickly, without thinking or filtering yourself, say to yourself out loud, "The emotion I am trying to block with sweets is ____________." Usually, once we hear it out loud, it does not seem so scary or worth blocking, and our desire for foods that lower our vibration disappears. Remember, it takes ninety days to set the pattern, so until you have eaten for ninety consecutive days on the Equilibrium Diet, you have not solidified your new pattern. If you "cheat" on day thirty, it is totally fine; it is just going to take you 120 days from when you began to completely set your pattern (ninety days after the sugar consumption). Another method that can help minimize the urge to eat fast foods or sweets is to know where you can find the healthy version or have a healthy version at home. Whole Foods sells dairy-free and sugar-free all-natural ice cream and some gluten-free, dairy-free, and sugar-free cookies. Know where to find them if you need them; you can also bake your own and freeze them.

What about portion sizes? How much of each food should I eat?

There are absolutely *no* restrictions on portion sizes. You can eat as much as you want of anything in the Equilibrium Diet as long as it is at the proper time of day: proteins before 2:00 p.m. and fruits after 2:00 p.m. Initially, you may feel like you are eating a ton of food, and you probably are; this is great. You are eating a lot because your nutritionally bankrupt body is so happy to finally be getting fed. After the first couple months, your desire for food may plummet; this is perfectly normal when the body swings away from its building cycle and toward a cleansing cycle. Above all, listen to your body. After ninety days on the Equilibrium Diet, you will know exactly what your body wants.

Do the fasting days in the program need to be done consecutively, or can I fast one day a week for ten weeks?

For the initial juice fast, I recommend a consecutive fast for at least three days and preferably seven to ten days. The first twenty-four hours of a fast are the hardest because the liver is still wondering about food and digestion. Then the liver goes into cleaning mode. Fasting experts will say that a three-day fast cleanses the colon; a five-day fast cleanses the blood; and a seven- to ten-day fast builds the immune system. The goal is to get as much toxic material out as quickly as possible so you immediately feel better and provide a clean break with your old lifestyle. After your initial fast, if you can and would like to fast one day a week or three days a month, that will definitely speed up the healing process. The point of the fast is to give you momentum and get the new pattern started.

I am a vegetarian. Should I try to eat organ meats?

This is up to you. If you are nutritionally depleted, like most people, organ meats are one of the easiest ways to build your foundation of health; however, for those who are vegetarians because they cringe at the idea of taking an animal's life, organ meats will not integrate well with their energy field. I tested one vegetarian for whom it physically and emotionally pained her vibration to eat an animal, so of course I advised her to avoid it. If possible, focus on raw dairy products, seaweeds and algae, and raw juices. Also be sure to properly prepare your grains, nuts, and seeds to minimize chelating your body's mineral stores with phytic acid.

I really don't like to exercise. Is the exercise component mandatory?

Nothing is ever mandatory. The exercise programs listed are low impact and based on *movement* and keeping the passages of elimination open and flowing. Do what you can and what feels good for the first ninety days; after that, if you do not want to exercise—don't! I am fairly active with my children, but I don't exercise *per se*. The diet and emotional healing is our top priority—exercise is simply a complementary activity to *help* you reach your goals.

I am thinking about trying the ninety-day program. Are you sure it will work if I try it?

Yes. This is the equivalent of asking if patching the holes in a leaky boat will make it more seaworthy. Or if revamping the engine will make it sail faster or more efficiently. The Equilibrium Diet is like running your body as a profitable company; you are using high-quality inputs (foods) and efficient processes (the timing of consumption). The goal of health is inevitable when we work *with* the body instead of against it.

Regarding the first enlightenment experience, why did the Jesus figure speak in English? Jesus never spoke English when he lived on earth. Why did you see Jesus and not God?

I only speak English, so perhaps the only way for God or Jesus to get through to me was to communicate in my language. Being all-knowing, perhaps God knew this and chose to speak in English. Alternatively, everything is information, and our brains filter all information. This filter is dictated by the constructs we allow to shape our thinking and beliefs: society, friends, family, likes and dislikes, and education. If we think of the brain as a computer program that is dictated by our subconscious, and if we consider all energy to be bits of information, then the program receives information and translates it to display the results of the program.

More than likely, my brain was picking up and running its preset programming on the information set that I was receiving. For instance, if I do not have any experience with jump ropes and see a jump rope for the first time in a shadowy room, I will probably filter the information to interpret it as a "snake." The enlightenment information set happened to best fit my *filter* of what "heaven or love or God energy" would be like. My brain program then displayed the results that I observed: a loud, booming voice and image of Jesus because that is what I associated with that set of information.

People with a "program" similar to mine would have a similar experience given the same information set. People with a different "program," perhaps someone with a Buddhist or Islamic background, would have a different reading or filtering of the information and hence a different output or experience. For instance, maybe they would have seen and heard the Buddha or Mohammed. Once the right brain receives the information, the left brain then translates the information we receive to be able to communicate it with others. For instance, when I *felt* the information about the state of universe, I literally *felt* it; there were no words. It was as if a zip file of information had been downloaded into me, and I felt it sitting there in my right brain. My left brain then went in and observed the *felt* information and tried to put words to translate it for other people to understand. This "left brain" translation occurs only to the extent we allow it. If a set of information is in direct conflict with our personal filter and belief system, then the conscious brain will block the information altogether in an attempt to protect itself. The more we relax our filters, the bigger and more magical the world and universe become.

How long did the entire experience of the first enlightenment last?

I had no sense of time during the experience. It was beyond time, but for perspective, the entire enlightenment experience from hearing Jesus's voice to the zap and download of information probably happened in less than thirty seconds. I am calculating this using the amount of time it takes to say the last two sentences of the Lord's Prayer.

Did the diet and lifestyle changes bring on the energetic awakening and enlightenment?

Yes—the dietary changes allowed the energy to begin flowing more efficiently through my body and energy systems. The Equilibrium Diet allowed my physical body to be in better communication with my higher energy bodies: the emotional, mental, and spiritual, which manifest physically as instincts.

This occurs as the physical body removes decades of toxic material. It becomes easier to sense the environment around you, because the energy is moving more freely between the physical body and the higher bodies, particularly emotions and thought forms. Many of the traditional Asian medicines describe the physical body as being shrouded in higher "subtle" energetic bodies.

Eating according to the Equilibrium Diet minimizes the stress on the liver, which is the most important detoxifying organ in the body. When the liver can process and clean more toxins than it takes in on a daily basis, dramatic health improvements occur. We have time to find and purge those old stuck emotions; eventually, we purge our genes. As the liver cleans, the blood flows more smoothly, the heart does not have to work as hard, the nervous system is not as stressed, and the mind and vision become clearer. The physical detoxification process and the mental detoxification process are one and the same—what one clears, the other clears.

Are there other factors not being taken into account in this analysis?

Did this enlightenment happen because of factors other than diet? Are ceteris paribus conditions present between when I began the diet and cleanses and experienced enlightenment? My external and internal environments were identical the entire time period with the exception of the dietary changes. There was no additional stress, no recreational drug use, no pharmaceutical drug use, and no change of jobs or location. Everything, literally everything, was the same, just as the Source wanted it. The Source knew that if anything else were different, my rational brain would use that as the "logical" explanation. We lived in the same house the entire time; I was attending graduate school the entire time; Lance worked at the same job the entire time; there were no deaths in the family. I could go on, but all of this equates to: ceteris paribus.

Is there life after death? Is there heaven?

This life is just a blip in the grand scheme of each of us. Each of us has always existed and will always exist. Human fears prevent us from remembering our truth, but as we peel back the layers of fear, we find ourselves—our true selves—and the one truth again. Then we *remember*: we are all connected. We have *always* existed, and we will *always* exist.

Who do you think Jesus was?

I see Jesus as being a vessel for the Source and living love in every moment. Jesus, Mary Magdalene, and other miracle workers come to remind us of our own Source and power. They come to inspire us to be our true selves and rise above the third dimension by fully *embodying* our earthly experience; good prophets remind us that we are all, in fact, prophets.

What religion are you?

I was raised around Christianity, spent most of my life as an atheist, and today I do not affiliate with any religion. Many religions put something between humans and Source, whether that is a god, goddess, or angelic being. Anything, absolutely anything, between us and Source is an illusion—which is of course, constructed of more Source! I do not go to church. I am my own church—I am spiritual. We are all humans, and that comes with a direct connection to the Creator and to the earth; it is not just a connection—it is—Creator, Source—that is all there is, and we are one and the same.

What does your husband say about all of this? Does he support you?

Lance and I serve as catalysts for each other. Lance's gallbladder illness and my research abilities catapulted us down the herbal and energetic paths initially, but there were times when one or both of us tried to slow down the quest for truth—always out of fear—and conflict would arise. We have experienced our twists and turns; we plodded on nonetheless, and Lance is completely supportive and loving of me being me. He and I both just want each other to be happy and fulfill our potential on Earth.

Your husband took many of the same steps you did; did he experience enlightenment too?

Yes, he did—though it came years after my first experience. Heaven, the Divine, and love can be experienced in infinite ways, because each individual carries different biases and beliefs that will slightly alter or filter each experience. We all experience exactly what we need to find ourselves and our highest paths. Lance is no different. The time difference in our experiences is directly related to how strictly we each adhered to the Equilibrium Diet and the number of fasting days. One day of juice fasting seems to remove as much toxic material as two to four weeks of eating according to the Equilibrium Diet. Lance also had lots of business meetings centered around lunch and dinner, so he ate out and ate meat at night a lot more than I did that first year.

* * *

Your Beginning

Our instincts and enlightenment are not a place. They are subtle. They are a state of being, a state where mind, body, and spirit all resonate in perfect harmony. Small differences fall away, and true acceptance emerges. Love is acceptance of all things, all traits, all ideas. It is also allowing ourselves and others to choose our own path.

Physically, enlightenment was a freeing sensation achieved no other way. It was a feeling of zero constraint—no body, no pain, no confinement, and no boundaries. I was one with everything and nothing, and it was the best experience of my life. It was so amazing that I spent two years of my life trying to recreate my experience of Source—I was addicted to the feeling of oneness. Finally, I snapped out of my enlightenment-seeking trance and realized there was nothing to seek—I was Source. I am Source. That's it! Literally, I was everything I had been seeking, and there was no one to pray to, or yell at, other than me. Shit. That's life changing. And that's when I stopped praying and started doing. I started making things how I wanted them to be—because when you are the most powerful, loving force in existence, that's what you do—*create*. And that is why we are all here, but that is another story for another day.

Thank you for letting me be a part of your journey. Writing this book took me in directions I had never *ever* planned on going. It opened doors that I would have been too afraid to open on my own. One of those doors made me realize that when we hide our true selves, we hurt ourselves—and we hurt others. Some of us venture out of hiding because we are sick of it; others venture out for those they love. Many of us recognize our unhealthy patterns and don't want to pass them down to our children. Now is the time to dig deep and leap—take the plunge and start your ninety-day program today!

You officially understand what equilibrium entails. Eating well takes effort and planning. But once you have done it and have seen yourself before and after, you will realize the benefits and will see how valuable you and your health really are. The continued choice to invest in yourself becomes easy. This, my friend, will be the adventure of a lifetime—perhaps many lifetimes—and you do not even have to leave your home. Choose to lose weight. Choose to look younger. Choose to return to health. Choose to know you are worth it. Choose to know yourself. Choose to invest ninety days in *yourself*, and you will *remember.*

Notes and References

Part 1

Chapter 2

1 For pictures and descriptions, see the Weston A. Price, DDS, book *Nutrition and Physical Degeneration*.

Chapter 5

1 See *Nutritional Healing from A to Z* by Bach.
2 See *Old Souls: The Scientific Evidence for Past Lives* (1999) by Tom Shroder.
3 Source: http://www.dcn.davis.ca.us/go/gizmo/1997/carol.html.
4 See *Many Lives, Many Masters* by Brian Weiss, as well as *Through Time into Healing* by Brian Weiss.

Chapter 9

1 The book *What to Expect When You Are Expecting* by Sharon Mazel and Heidi Murkoff documents several cases of sympathy bloating, weight gain, fatigue, headaches, and morning sickness.
2 See Pearce's book *The Magical Child* for more on his findings.

Part 2

Chapter 15

1 A 2002 study titled "Enhancement of the chemoprotective enzymes glucuronosyl transferase and glutathione transferase in specific organs of the rat by the coffee components kahweol and cafestol," by Huber, Prustomersky, Delbanco, Uhl, Scharf,

Turesky, Thier, and Schulte-Hermann, finds similar results to the German trials. It can be found at http://www.ncbi.nlm.nih.gov/pubmed/12029384.

Chapter 16

1 See Weston A. Price, DDS, *Nutrition and Physical Degeneration* for studies and pictures on each of the fat-soluble vitamin deficiencies.

2 In general, Nourishing Traditions does an excellent job in recommended food preparations and follows the ancient and primitive traditions that are best for digestion and absorption.

3 For the science behind the pH cycle of the body, read *The Pro-Vita Diet* by Jack Tipps, NE PhD.

4 For the science behind the pH cycle of the body, read *The Pro-Vita Diet* by Jack Tipps, NE PhD.

5 For the full discussion on primitive diets, see Weston A. Price, DDS, *Nutrition and Physical Degeneration.*

Chapter 17

1 See *The Yeast Connection* by William G. Crook, ND, for a full discussion of candida overgrowth and the vast majority of people affected by it.

2 I have seen one exception to the general finding of people being able to digest raw goat's milk more easily than raw cow's milk. One elderly man I vibrationally tested was very strong for raw cow's milk but weak for goat milk. He was a cancer patient of many years and many different medical therapies and also tested very strongly for intravenous glutathione. Raw cow's milk happens to be high in usable glutathione.

3 For some data on the relative safety of raw milk go to: http://www.westonaprice.org/press/government-data-proves-raw-milk-safe/.

4 See *The Ultimate Healing System* by Donald Lepore, ND, for a full analysis.

5 See The Price Foundation, www.westonprice.org, or Weston A. Price's book, *Nutrition and Physical Degeneration.*

6 For a summary of Irina Ermakova's GMO soy results see: http://www.gmfreecymru.org/pivotal_papers/ermakova.htm. And for more information go to www.responsibletechnology.org.

7 For the full study and discussion see the 1997 report *Depression of Lymphocyte Transformation Following Oral Glucose Ingestion,* by Kathleen M. Nauss, PhD, Stephen Alpert, MD, and Robert M. Suskind, MD, which can be found at http://www.sciencedirect.com/science/article/pii/s0271531784800573. Also see the 1970s research by Dr. Linus Pauling, which is documented in many places, including: http://alternativehealthatlanta.com/immune-system/sugar-and-your-immune-system/.

Chapter 18

[1] The three doshas or constitution types in Ayurvedic medicine are vata, pitta, and kapha.

Chapter 21

[1] See the full story at http://www.howtofast.net/spiritual/christianity.html.

Chapter 22

[1] For an interesting discussion, read *The Amazing Liver and Gallbladder Flush* by Andreas Moritz.

CPSIA information can be obtained
at www.ICGtesting.com
Printed in the USA
LVOW08s2104030417
529439LV00003BA/800/P

9 781504 369022